The Philippines

The Philippines

BY WALTER OLEKSY

Enchantment of the World
Second Series

Children's Press®

A Division of Grolier Publishing

NEW YORK   LONDON   HONG KONG   SYDNEY
DANBURY, CONNECTICUT

Frontispiece: Boys riding a water buffalo

Consultant: Janet Bauer, Ph. D., Associate Professor of International Studies
and Assistant Director of the Trinity Center for Collaborative
Teaching and Research, Trinity College

Please note: All statistics are as up-to-date as possible at the time of publication.

Visit Children's Press on the Internet: http://publishing.grolier.com

Book design by Ox and Company, Inc.

Library of Congress Cataloging-in-Publication Data

Oleksy, Walter G., 1930–
         The Philippines / by Walter Oleksy.
             p.   cm.   —   (Enchantment of the world. Second series)
         Includes bibliographical references and index.
         Summary: Describes the geography, plants, animals, history,
economy, language, religions, culture, sports, arts, and people of
the Philippines.
         ISBN 0-516-21010-6
         1. Philippines—Juvenile literature. [1. The Philippines.]
I. Title. II. Series.
DS655.043 2000
959.9—dc21   99-13701
                                                                    CIP

Acknowledgments

I met some very friendly and helpful Filipinos while research-
ing and writing this book. The Philippines Consul General in
Chicago, Emelinda Lee-Pineda, and her staff provided a lot of
help. Beth Hernandez, a Chicagoan whose relatives live in the
Philippines, helped me interview Filipinos via e-mail. Kelly
Griggs, who manages the Teen Exchange website for The
Mining Company, put me in touch with young Filipinos for
on-line conversations to learn more about their lives in the
Philippines.

Contents

Cover photo:
Miniloc Island lagoon

CHAPTER

A mangrove swamp

A starfish

Where East Meets West

8

The beautiful Philippine Islands are a tropical paradise in the southwest Pacific Ocean. The Philippines is one of the few countries on Earth today where the present and the distant past coexist in harmony. Here you can enjoy all the comforts and excitement of a modern coastal city where millions of people live and work. Then, in less than an hour, you can walk in the mountains where people still live as their ancestors did—not just 200 years ago but as far back as the Stone Age.

The business district in Manila is modern and lively.

Life in the Philippines has been influenced by a variety of cultures including Chinese, Japanese, and Malaysian, as well as American. As a result, the country is a melting pot of ethnic groups from Asia, the Pacific, and the West.

One generalization, however, may be made about the Philippines and the Filipinos. It would be hard to find a friendlier place or friendlier people. For many Filipinos, life seems to be a healthy balance of work and play. They have a positive

Opposite: **The Pacific War Memorial represents an eternal flame.**

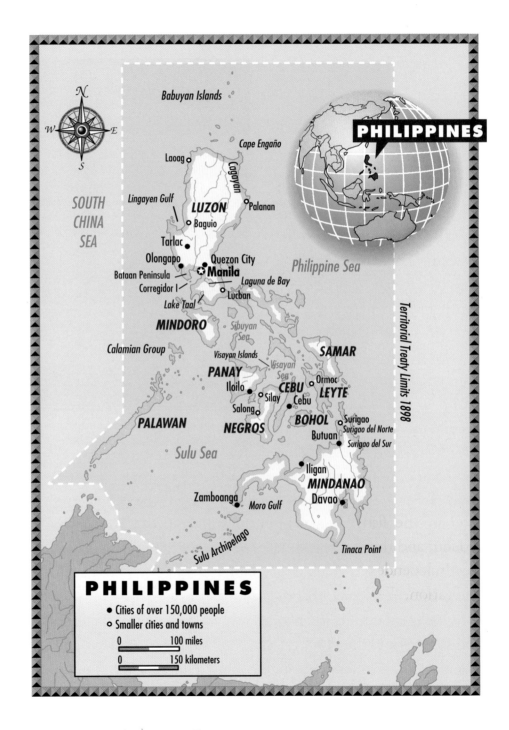

Babuyan Islands

Cape Engaño

Laoag

Cagayan

LUZON

Palanan

SOUTH CHINA SEA

Lingayen Gulf

Baguio

Tarlac

Olongapo

Quezon City

Manila

Bataan Peninsula

Corregidor I

Laguna de Bay

Lucban

Lake Taal

Philippine Sea

MINDORO

Sibuyan Sea

Calamian Group

Visayan Islands

SAMAR

PANAY

Visayan Sea

Iloilo

CEBU

Ormoc

LEYTE

Silay

Cebu

Salong

BOHOL

Surigao

Surigao del Norte

PALAWAN

NEGROS

Butuan

Surigao del Sur

Sulu Sea

Iligan

MINDANAO

Zamboanga

Moro Gulf

Davao

Sulu Archipelago

Tinaca Point

Territorial Treaty Limits 1898

PHILIPPINES

PHILIPPINES

- Cities of over 150,000 people
- Smaller cities and towns

| 0 | 100 miles |
| 0 | 150 kilometers |

School students in Pampanga show their friendly nature.

outlook and a strong faith, and—most of the time—the sun shines, the fish bite, the pineapples ripen, it's warm year-round, and the surf is up.

Independent today, after hundreds of years of Western colonization, Filipinos embrace the best of the West while keeping the best of the East, blending modern life with the rich cultural heritage of the past. Their role as island stepping stones between West and East makes the Philippines a fascinating country to live in—and to visit.

The Pearl of the Orient Sea

Pangulasian Island

About a hundred years ago, José Rizal, a leader in the Philippines' struggle for independence from Spain, described his island country in Southeast Asia as the "Pearl of the Orient Sea." The Philippine Islands form an *archipelago*—an island group—that looks like a necklace of beautiful gems set in the vast blue Pacific Ocean.

Land of Beauty and Contrasts

The Republic of the Philippines, an island country lying about 500 miles (805 km) from mainland Asia, is a group of 7,107 islands that stretch across 115,839 square miles (300,000 sq km) of the western edge of the Pacific Ocean. It is one of the world's largest archipelagoes.

The South China Sea lies north and west of the Philippines. The island of Taiwan, or Nationalist China, lies

Opposite: **Lalaguna Beach in the Mindoro Province**

PEOPLE'S REPUBLIC OF CHINA

TAIWAN

0   100 mi.

0   150 km.

South China Sea

Babuyan Islands

PACIFIC OCEAN

LUZON — SIERRA MADRE

ZAMBALES MTNS.

Philippine Sea

Mt. Pinatubo ▲

✪ **Manila**

Mayon Volcano ▲

Philippine Trench

PALAWAN   *Sulu Sea*

MINDANAO

Zamboanga ●   ● Davao

Mt. Apo ▲

Borneo

Sulu Archipelago

Celebes Sea

Sulawesi

Ocean Depth

0	650	6,500	13,000	20,000	26,000	Feet

0	200	2,000	4,000	6,000	8,000	Meters

beyond the South China Sea to the north. The People's Republic of China is to the northwest, and Vietnam lies to the west. Malaysia is southwest of the Philippines, and Indonesia lies to the southwest and south. The Pacific Ocean is directly east of the Philippines beyond the Philippine Sea.

The Philippine Islands extend 1,152 miles (1,854 km) from north to south and 688 miles (1,107 km) from east to west. Sixty-five percent of the islands' total landmass is mountainous, so most of its 76 million people live crowded in the valleys and along the coastlines.

The Philippines' Geographical Features

Largest Island: Luzon, 40,420 square miles (104,680 sq km)

Smallest Island: Unknown; one of more than 642 very small islands

Coastline: 22,554 miles (36,296 km)

Largest City: Manila, population 10.4 million (1997 est.)

Longest River: Cagayan River, Luzon, 220 miles (354 km)

Largest Lake: Laguna de Bay, Luzon, 344 square miles (891 sq km)

Highest Elevation: Mount Apo, 9,692 feet (2,954 m)

Lowest Elevation: Sea level

Average Temperature: May–June, 82–92°F (28–33°C); December–January, 75–84°F (24–29°C)

Average Rainfall: From 35 to 216 inches (89 to 549 cm)

Average Number of Typhoons per Year: Five to twelve

In total land area, the Philippines is slightly larger than the state of Arizona. It is also a little larger than another island nation, the United Kingdom—England, Scotland, Wales, and Northern Ireland—which totals 93,602 square miles (242,410 sq km). Physically, the two nations are very different because the Philippines is not in the cooler Northern Hemisphere but in the warm, sunny tropics.

The Philippines is rich in natural resources, especially copper, gold, iron, nickel, and coal. Until recent years, the islands' economy depended mainly on agriculture, but a greater emphasis on manufacturing, especially in high technology, has created a more varied and stronger economy.

When seen from above in an airplane, the Philippines is a series of beautiful green islands with many mountains. The land slopes down from the mountains to cultivated terraces and plains, and a sandy or rocky coastline. Some of the larger islands have small lakes and rivers.

The Philippine Islands vary in size and population.

Most of the islands are small. Only about 150 of them are larger than 5 square miles (13 sq km). Eleven of the largest islands have about 95 percent of the country's total land area. The nation's major businesses and industries are on these islands, and most of the Filipino people live there.

Only about one-third of the Philippine Islands are inhabited, and just 2,773 of them have names. About 19 percent of the land is suitable for farming, another 12 percent has permanent crops, 4 percent has meadows and grazing land, 46 percent is made up of forests and woodland, and the remaining 19 percent has other uses.

A Land in Motion

The Philippine Islands were formed centuries ago by volcanic action and movements of the earth's crust. Like all islands, they are actually the tops of underwater mountains that are still being formed by occasional volcanic action and earthquakes.

Many thousands of years ago, the Philippine Islands and the island of Borneo were connected by land to each other and to mainland Asia. People, animals, and plant life traveled among the areas across "land bridges." After the Ice Age, the sea level rose as the ice melted. The ocean then covered most of the low-lying land among the areas except the islands that are there today.

Mountain ranges are found throughout the Philippines. Their lower slopes and the narrow strips of land along the coastal plains provide rich farming land. Large expanses of level land are rare in the Philippines. However, nearly half of the total land area could be farmed by terracing. In terracing, farmers build wide flat ridges on hillsides.

Dense forests once covered most of the Philippines, but extensive lumbering, which began in the 1950s, has destroyed most of the woodlands. This deforestation made room for more farms, houses, and businesses. Like many other countries, the Philippines has sacrificed some of its natural beauty in the name of progress.

Dangers in Paradise

When the sun shines and the weather is good, the Philippines is still a paradise. But it is a land of changeable weather. In addition, volcanic eruptions, earthquakes, and typhoons sometimes cause widespread death and destruction.

The Philippines lies within the tropics, so the climate is humid and ranges from warm to hot. The average year-round temperature in the lowlands is 80°F (27°C), but it is much cooler in the mountains. Humidity varies between 71 and 85 percent. Average annual rainfall ranges from 35 to 216 inches (89 to 549 cm).

The weather changes according to the direction of the monsoon winds. These winds, which affect much of southern Asia, change direction with the seasons. Northeast monsoons bring dry, warm weather from November to May. Southwest monsoons bring rain from June to October, with July and August being the wettest months.

The Philippines have a rainy season from July through November and a dry season from January to June. Days are usually warm, cooled somewhat by sea breezes. From November to February, the islands enjoy warm, sunny days and slightly cooler nights. The hottest months are March, April, and May, when temperatures range from 86°F (30°C) to 97°F (36°C).

The Drought of 1998

The monsoons that usually sweep through Southeast Asia failed to come in the summer of 1998. As a result, the region, including the Philippines, suffered its worst drought in fifty years.

Not only were crops lost to the dry spell, but 1.9 million acres (769,000 ha) of forest and farmland were destroyed in fires. Thousands of Filipino farmers went hungry when their crops dried up or burned. The drought added to Asia's economic slump, which began to threaten the economy of the rest of the world.

The destruction caused by a major typhoon

Each year between June and November, from five to twelve or more typhoons—tropical cyclones known locally as *bagulos*—lash the Philippine Islands. The large, slow-moving storms come from the southeast bringing heavy rains, mainly to northern Luzon and the eastern Visayan Islands. Flooding and winds up to 150 miles (241 km) per hour cause widespread damage and loss of life.

In 1991, a violent typhoon caused torrents of water to thunder down from the mountains over the village of Ormoc on the island of Leyte, leaving 3,000 people dead and 50,000 homeless. The effects of the typhoon were worse because of deforestation in the region.

Most of the larger islands in the Philippines are capped by volcanic mountains. Some 21 of the country's volcanoes are active and erupt periodically, while another 200 are dor-

Mount Pinatubo Erupts

The worst volcanic eruption in the Philippines in recent years occurred in 1991. Mount Pinatubo on the island of Luzon erupted, causing widespread damage. More than 800 people died and volcanic lava and ash destroyed crops and towns. The weather was affected worldwide. Clark Air Base, a U.S. military facility on Luzon, was buried under ash and had to be abandoned.

mant. While volcanic action is destructive, it also enriches the soil with ash, so the farmers grow a great variety of crops.

The Philippines lies in what is called the "earthquake belt" of the Pacific Ocean. An average of one earthquake measuring at least 7.75 on the Richter scale and seven quakes measuring 7.0–7.4 occur in the islands every ten years. Five earthquakes measuring 6.0–6.9 on the Richter scale occur every year. Volcanoes also erupt frequently in the region.

The Pacific Ring of Fire

- **Volcanoes, Ring of Fire**
— **Tectonic Plates**

The Philippines at a Glance

The Philippine Islands are composed of two large islands and a group of smaller islands in between. Luzon, the largest and most populated island in the Philippines at 40,420 square miles (104,680 sq km), is at the northern end of the island chain. Mindanao, which is 36,537 square miles (94,624 sq km), is at the southern end. Between the two lie the Visayan Islands, made up of about 7,000 islands.

Two of the Philippines' major cities are in the northern group of islands—Manila, the capital and the center of politics and government, and adjoining Quezon City. Manila and Quezon City, along with smaller cities in the area, make up Metro Manila, home to more than 12 million people at the end of the twentieth century. The southern group of islands holds 9 of the 11 largest islands in the Philippines, including Mindanao and the Sulu Archipelago, a group of about 400 islands that extend toward Borneo.

West of the main body of islands lies Palawan Island, a narrow strip of mountainous territory. About one-fourth of the Philippine archipelago's islands and islets are found in the Palawan Province. Palawan is a province of breathtaking natural beauty including jungles, rain forests, wilderness, and miles of pristine beaches. This largely undeveloped island is rich in sea life, spectacular underwater gardens, wild orchids, birds, butterflies, and rare animals. Many people consider Palawan the Philippines' last frontier.

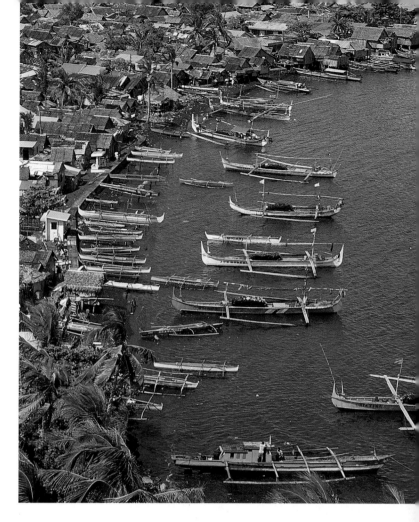

Fishing boats docked at Luzon Island

Luzon

Luzon occupies about one-third of the nation's total land area and has about half of its population. This island is the Philippines' leading industrial and agricultural center.

Northern Luzon is dominated by two parallel mountain ranges that run north to south. They are separated by the Cagayan Valley with its fertile Central Plain, the nation's broadest expanse of level land and a major rice-growing region. Southern Luzon is much narrower though also mountainous, with fertile soil covering its slopes and plains.

Opposite: **A lagoon in the Palawan Province**

Mayon Volcano

Mount Mayon in southeastern Luzon is the "queen of Philippine volcanoes." The name *Mayon* means "beautiful" in the Bicol language. Rising from fertile farmland to a majestic 8,077 feet (2,462 m), the volcano has retained its perfect cone shape, even after thirty-three eruptions over the past 150 years. It last erupted in 1993, killing more than 60 residents.

Manila, the nation's capital and largest city, is a sprawling city on Manila Bay, a 770-square-mile (1,994-sq-km) inlet of the South China Sea on Luzon's southwestern coast. Corregidor Island is at the inlet's mouth. Its strategic location has made Manila the nation's commercial and financial center, as well as its principal port city.

It is said that the heart of the Philippines beats in Metro Manila. This metropolis, which comprises four cities (Manila, Quezon City, Pasay, and Calookan) plus nearby small towns, is the seat of the national government, the center of arts and education, and the nation's commercial, industrial, business, and financial hub. Skyscrapers and expensive new homes are always going up in Metro Manila. Metro Manila is soon expected to span the entire width of Luzon and become one of the largest city networks in Asia.

Metro Manila is the center of business and industry, as well as of arts and education.

Students enjoy the courtyard of the San Agustin Church of Intramuros.

A housing complex in Tondo, a crowded lower-income community in Manila

The Pasig River divides Manila in half. Intramuros, an old walled city built by the Spanish, lies south of the river. North of the river is Tondo, a crowded lower-income community.

Several mountain ranges run through Luzon, including the Sierra Madre. They extend for about 215 miles (346 km) along the northeastern coast and range in height from 3,500 to 5,000 feet (1,067 to 1,524 m). The rolling plains of the Cagayan River Valley lie between the Sierra Madre and the Cordillera Central, whose highest peak is 9,606 feet (2,928 m). The central plains of Luzon extend westward to the Zambales Mountains, a smaller chain that slopes southward into the Bataan Peninsula.

Looking at the Philippines' Cities

Quezon City, the nation's capital from 1948 until 1976, borders Manila on the northeast. Although Manila is now the capital of the Philippines, many government offices still operate from Quezon City. The central campus of the University of the Philippines is also located there. Almost 2 million people live in Quezon City.

Cebu City, the oldest Spanish town in the Philippines, is a business and industrial center today, second only to Manila in economic importance. With 3.1 million residents, Cebu City also is one of the most densely populated cities in the islands, even though central mountains as high as 3,324 feet (1,013 m) run the length of Cebu Island.

Davao, the largest city in Mindanao, has a population of 1.3 million. It has become a melting pot for people from other parts of the islands.

The city of Baguio rests on a 4,500-foot- (1,372-m-) high plateau of the Cordillera Central Mountains. Resorts nestled in its pine forests—and its cooler temperatures—make it a popular vacation retreat.

The Visayan Islands

About 7,000 islands, including seven of the largest, make up the Visayan Islands in the shallow waters of the central part of the Philippines. People who live in bustling Luzon enjoy the slower pace of the southern islands with their calm waters and palm-lined beaches. Boys still shimmy up coconut trees for fresh coconuts there, and women tend slow fires for the noon-day meal. At dusk, fishers push their outriggers off into the sea for some night-fishing. Blue-finned tuna, red snappers, lobsters, crabs, and giant prawns are plentiful.

Samar, in the east, has low, rugged mountains and dense rain forests. It receives heavy rainfall from typhoons each year. Leyte, in the west, has central mountains rising to 4,426 feet (1,349 m).

The market at a shopping center on Negros Island

The white beaches of Boracay Island are considered some of the most beautiful in the Philippines.

Cebu is a long, narrow island in the center of the Visayan group. Negros Island, to the west of Cebu, is largely mountainous. Its highest peak is Canlaon Volcano, which is 8,070 feet (2,460 m) above sea level. Its volcanic lava has enriched the soil for sugar and other farming.

Panay, west of Negros, is the westernmost of the Visayan Islands. The mountains along its western coast include the lofty Mount Nangtud at 6,724 feet (2,049 m).

Many people consider Boracay, in the Viscayan province of Aklan, to be the most beautiful of all the islands. Boracay is only about 4 miles (6.4 km) wide and 10 miles (16 km) long. Shaped like a butterfly, it lies in a gentle sea amid abundant coral reefs. Coconut trees sway in the breeze, and rare *puka* coral shells can be found on its white sand beaches.

Mindanao

Southernmost Mindanao is the second-largest island in the Philippines, after Luzon. The varied topography of Mindanao includes large peninsulas and five mountain systems. The island has green valleys, swift-flowing rivers, smooth lakes, forests, and waterfalls, as well as mangrove swamps, lowlands, and marshes.

One of the deepest places in the world is the Philippine Trench, off the northeast coast of Mindanao. This huge depression in the Philippine Sea is 6.5 miles (10.5 km) below the surface of the Pacific Ocean. The highest mountain in the Philippines at 9,692 feet (2,954 m), Mount Apo is an active volcano near the city of Davao.

The region is rich in minerals, with about 80 percent of the nation's iron reserves and all of its nickel. Local farms produce more than half of the national output of pineapple, corn, coffee, cocoa, and abaca—a bananalike plant whose trunks are ripped lengthwise and made into rope.

A rain forest on Mindanao

Mindanao is unique in several ways. It is home to one of the most isolated and obscure tribes in the world—the Tasaday. Davao is the largest city in the world in terms of area. Surigao has the world's richest nickel deposits as well as the *Gloria maris*, one of the most expensive seashells on earth. It is also home to the world's second-largest eagle—the Philippine eagle.

Rivers and Lakes

The Philippines has many rivers. Most are on Luzon and Mindanao and are swift but short. The longest and most navigable rivers in Luzon are the 220-mile (354-km) Cagayan River in northern Luzon and the 120-mile (193-km) Pampanga River, which flows into Manila Bay. The Pampanga's waters irrigate the fertile Central Plains, one of the most important farming areas in the Philippines. The Agusan River in eastern Mindanao extends 240 miles (386 km) northward to Butuan Bay and irrigates large crops of rice and corn in a fertile valley 50 miles (80 km) wide.

The Philippines has many small lakes, but only three large bodies of inland water. The nation's largest lake, 344-square-mile (891-sq-km) Laguna de Bay, is in central Luzon near Manila. Lake Lanao, on Mindanao, is the second-largest lake, covering 131 square miles (339 sq km). Forty miles (64 km) south of Manila, Lake Taal sits in the top of a dead volcano. A small island in the center of the 94-square-mile (243-sq-km) lake is an active volcano.

Opposite: **Lake Sebu is an inland sea in the Southern Tiruray Highlands.**

Wildlife in a Modern Paradise

L IKE MOST TROPICAL LANDS, THE PHILIPPINES HAS A WIDE variety of plants and animals, and its waters are full of many species of fish. Although 76 million people live on the islands, conservationists work hard to preserve the archipelago's wildlife and the environment that sustains it.

Opposite: **Bougainvillea flowers have woody vines and purple or red petals.**

Plant Life for Beauty and Food

Fertile volcanic soil and abundant sunshine and rain give the Philippines a great variety of plant life, from 1,000 species of ferns to about 3,000 kinds of trees. Many of the plants originally came from Malaysia and Indonesia, and even from distant Australia.

Rice is the Philippines' most important crop, so rice fields thrive on the islands. Coffee plantations are found in the high

Orchids in the Tropics

The sweetly scented Sampaguita orchid is the national flower. It has tiny fragrant white petals, and several flowers are strung together in garlands.

More than 800 species of exotic orchids thrive in the rain forests and mangrove swamps of the Philippines. Many orchids are named after insects and animals, such as the butterfly, spider, and lizard orchids. One of the rarest species, the *waling-waling* of Davao, blooms only once a year. Like Hawaiians, Filipinos welcome visitors with leis (necklaces made of flowers) and orchid corsages.

Wildlife in a Modern Paradise **31**

levels of the Batangas Province of Luzon and on the mountainsides of Mindanao. Cacao, which is used to make cocoa and other chocolate products, is grown mainly in the southern parts of the Sulu Archipelago and in the Cagayan Valley in northern Luzon.

The coconuts, pineapples, papayas, cassavas, and melons that grow on the islands are sold at open-air markets. Many varieties of bananas grow throughout the islands, ranging in size from little "ladyfingers" to the large Sabas.

Thick groves of bamboo, a fast-growing woody grass, are also found throughout the islands. Bamboo is used for a wide variety of purposes, such as building houses, bridges, fences, furniture, and fish traps; weaving baskets and hats; and making flutes.

The Tree of Life

One of the most abundant and important trees in the Philippines is the coconut palm. Every part of this tree is used, so it is no wonder Filipinos call it the "Tree of Life."

The branches are used for shelter, the nectar of the flowers provides a sweet drink, the coconuts are used for food and drink, the husks provide many useful products, and the trunk is cut into lumber. Many Filipino families plant a coconut tree to commemorate the birth of a child.

Energetic boys and girls like to scramble up a coconut tree, their bare feet fitting into the notches in the trunk. When they reach the top, they cut off a coconut with a sharp knife and drink its juice.

Cogon, a type of wild grass, covers about 18 percent of the land in the Philippines. Rattan and palm trees thrive in the forests that cover over 40 percent of the land and have many commercial uses. Mats, bags, and hats are woven from the leaves of the buri palm, and spear handles, walking sticks, and fishing rods are made from the palma brava, or *anahaw*.

Evergreen forests, mainly pine, are commonly found in the lowland areas and on the mountainsides up to 2,000 feet (610 m) where there is sufficient rainfall. Also widespread are stands of Philippine mahogany trees that grow to enormous size.

Mangrove trees grow abundantly in swamps along the coastlines. They provide firewood for people in coastal villages.

Bamboo was used to form a dock in the Pagsanjan Falls of Luzon.

Narra, the National Tree

The Philippines' national tree, the narra, grows in the cities as well as in the lowland rain forests. Its yellow flowers brighten the streets in March and April, while its hardwood is used in making furniture and for wood carvings.

A mangrove swamp at sunset

Molave forests are found in areas that have distinct wet and dry seasons. Molave trees, which have hard, yellow wood, belong to the teak family. Banyan trees, members of the mulberry family, are also abundant. Beneath the shade of rain-forest treetops are many vines; epiphytes, or air plants; and climbing palm trees.

Wildlife of the Tropics

The Philippines has few mammals or other wild animals. The largest wild animal in the archipelago is the ferocious tamarau, found on the mountains of Mindoro. It is a dwarf variety of the domestic water buffalo (carabao), which is widely used on the islands' farms for plowing and hauling.

Outside of tamarau, water buffalo, wild pigs, and jungle boar, most of the 233 species of animals in the Philippines are small. Wildcats include palm civets, the rare Palawan bear cat, and the leopard cat found on Palawan, Panay, Negros, and Cebu.

A variety of flying lemurs and other species of monkeys, mainly macaques, live in the forests too. The very cute and clever mouse deer lives on Palawan Island. The archipelago also has many squirrels, mongooses, shrews, porcupines, and skunks; dozens of kinds of rodents including swamp rats; and fifty-seven species of bats.

A leopard cat

Several animal species on the archipelago are endangered because deforestation, hunting, and urban development threaten their habitat. They include the tamarau and the mouse deer; Koch's pitta, a deep-forest bird; the pelican; the tarsier; and the sarus crane.

Crocodiles, once widespread in the Philippines, are now almost extinct, found only in remote regions of Palawan and Mindanao. The king cobra is found on Palawan, while pythons, water snakes, and other varieties of snakes are common throughout the islands. Large monitor lizards are also plentiful in the countryside. Geckos, small lizards that have a loud, distinctive call, are common in the islands. Geckos are welcome in many homes because they keep the house free of insects, so many boys and girls keep them as pets.

The mouse deer

Tarsier Monkeys

Tiny owl-eyed tarsiers, called the world's smallest monkeys, live mostly in the rain forests of Bohol, Leyte, and Mindanao. Nocturnal primates, they have large eyes to enable them to see well at night when they are most active in pursuit of food—mainly insects, lizards, frogs, and small birds. They are believed to have come from India centuries ago.

Birds of Beauty and Prey

The Philippine eagle is the archipelago's national emblem. It is the world's second-largest eagle species, after the South American harpy eagle. It was once known as the "monkey-eating eagle," but today it mainly hunts flying squirrels and monitor lizards in its forest habitat. It is also the world's most endangered eagle because of hunting and the encroachment of loggers and farmers on its habitat. Only about 200 of these magnificent birds survive today, despite a breeding program to increase their number.

There are more than 500 species of tropical birds in the Philippines, and 145 of them are found nowhere else. Another 160 migrant species come to the islands to escape the northeast Asian winter.

The most common birds in the archipelago are the Philippine cockatoo, the Philippine hawk, the Philippine mallard, the wandering whistling duck, the great scops owl, the bleeding-heart pigeon, the nutmeg imperial pigeon, and the *siete colores* (seven colors) pigeon.

The largest bird, more than 3 feet (1 m) tall, is the rare eastern sarus, or Sharpe's crane, found in the swamps of the Cagayan Valley, the Central Plain, and Bicol. The archipelago is also home to the world's smallest falcon—the Philippine falconet, or pygmy falcon.

The many rare bird species that live on Palawan include the beautiful Palawan peacock pheasant, which is also threatened by hunting and trapping. Brightly colored parrots are mainly found on Palawan, and many of them are exported as pets.

Opposite: **The Philippine eagle is the world's second-largest eagle.**

Seas Rich with Marine Life

As lush and pleasing as these islands are, many people consider the underwater landscapes of the Philippines even more beautiful. Reefs teem with small fish in an amazing variety of shapes and colors, while the surrounding waters hold dolphins, whales, jellyfish, sea anemones, sponges, and starfish. Divers also often see sharks, rays, moray eels, and sea snakes.

The warm seas around the Philippines abound with fish, including *Pondoka pygmaea*, the world's smallest fish. About 750 species of these fish are suitable for eating. The most abundant are tuna, anchovies, sardines, herring, mackerel,

A starfish on a reef in the Mindoro Strait

Shell-Collectors' Paradise

The Philippines is one of the world's richest shellfish habitats. Over 21,000 of the 100,000 shellfish species known worldwide are found in the archipelago. Filipinos dive in the seas for shells or find them on the beaches and use them for their own jewelry or sell them for export. Some shell specimens are worth thousands of dollars.

grouper, and sea bass. There are also lobster, shrimp, crab, and snappers, as well as green turtles and mollusks. The Filipino diet is based on cooked rice and fish—a main source of protein. Sport fishers catch swordfish, sailfish, and marlin.

Pearl oysters, found mainly in the Sulu Archipelago, produce pearls of great beauty. The "Pearl of Allah," the world's largest natural pearl, was found in a giant clam off Palawan in 1934 and is valued at more than $30 million.

A Long Struggle for Independence

BROTHERS IN ARMS
IN THESE HALLOWED SURROUNDINGS WHERE HEROES SLEEP
MAY THEIR ASHES SCATTER WITH THE WIND AND LIVE IN THE HEARTS OF
THOSE WHO WERE LEFT BEHIND.
THEY DIED FOR FREEDOM'S RIGHT AND IN HEAVEN'S SIGHT
THEIRS WAS A NOBLE CAUSE.

THE FIRST PEOPLE WHO LIVED IN THE PHILIPPINES PROBABLY came to the islands from Southeast Asia over land bridges that existed more than 30,000 years ago. Fishers and farmers from Indonesia and Malaysia are believed to have arrived by ship about 3000 B.C. and settled along the coasts. Some moved inland and formed their own settlements, and each group developed its own culture and language. Today, the Philippines remains a land of many cultures and languages.

In the A.D. 1200s, ten boats called *datu* (meaning "chieftain") sailed from Borneo, each carrying 100 men. They landed on what is now Panay Island in the Visayas to start a new community.

Later settlers lived in communities called *barangay*, after the name of the ships on which they came. They established an advanced civilization based on rice, fishing, weaving, mining, and trading. They used shells for money, wrote on bamboo, had a set of laws, and were governed by a council of their elders. They worshiped their ancestors and nature. However, the groups fought with one another, and their lack of unity made them easy prey for Spanish conquest.

In 1493, Pope Alexander VI issued a decree that would have a devastating impact on the Philippines, although he did

Opposite: **A Pacific war monument to U.S. and Filipino soldiers**

not even know the archipelago existed. He divided all past and future discoveries in the New World between Portugal and Spain, assigning discoveries of Atlantic Ocean land west of the Azores to Spain. The Azores lie 800 miles (1,287 km) west of Portugal.

A Portuguese navigator, Ferdinand Magellan, wanted to sail westward across the Atlantic Ocean to find the Spice Islands of the East Indies. The king of Portugal refused to pay for the expedition, so Magellan began his journey in 1519 in the service of Spain.

Magellan became the first known European to reach the Philippines. He anchored near Samar on March 17, 1521, and landed at Cebu on April 7, claiming all the islands for Spain. However, after only a few weeks in the Philippines, he was killed while taking sides in a battle between warring chiefs, and his men departed without establishing a settlement.

Ferdinand Magellan

First Journey Around the World

Ferdinand Magellan's historic journey to the Philippines led to the discovery that the world is round and not flat. He captained most of the first voyage around the world, one of the greatest achievements in navigation.

Magellan left Spain with five ships, but two sank on the voyage to the Philippines. One of the three remaining ships was lost in a battle with Philippine natives. The two ships that were left sailed for Spain, but only one, commanded by Juan Sebastian del Cano, made it back.

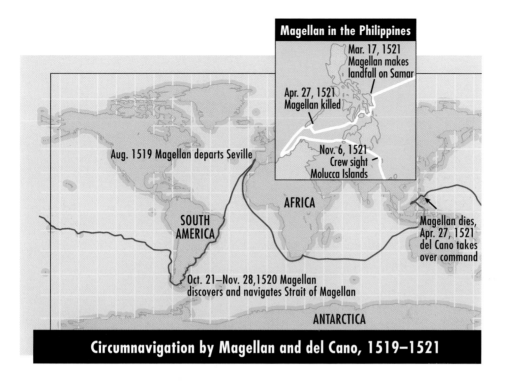

Magellan in the Philippines

Mar. 17, 1521
Magellan makes
landfall on Samar

Apr. 27, 1521
Magellan killed

Nov. 6, 1521
Crew sight
Molucca Islands

Aug. 1519 Magellan departs Seville

AFRICA

SOUTH
AMERICA

Magellan dies,
Apr. 27, 1521
del Cano takes
over command

Oct. 21–Nov. 28,1520 Magellan
discovers and navigates Strait of Magellan

ANTARCTICA

Circumnavigation by Magellan and del Cano, 1519–1521

Spanish Conquest

The Philippine Islands were again claimed by Spain in 1543, by Ruy Lopez de Villalobos and his expedition. He named the archipelago *Islas Filipinas* in honor of Prince Felipe, later King Philip II of Spain.

The first permanent Spanish colonial occupation of the islands began, however, in 1565 when another group of Spanish explorers established a fort and church on Cebu. They were led by General Miguel Lopez de Legazpi, a conquistador who had helped impose harsh Spanish rule on Mexico.

A Spanish settlement was established, and Legazpi and his followers divided the land among themselves. They virtually made slaves of the natives, whom they called "Indios," forcing them to work as tenant farmers, laborers, and servants on

Spanish colonial houses
in Manila

what had been their own land. While the lowlands were being colonized, head-hunting tribes fled, hiding in the mountains where many of their descendants live today, although they no longer practice head-hunting.

Spanish priests, meanwhile, converted most of the Filipinos to Roman Catholicism. In the same period, Muslim missionaries spread the faith of Islam in Luzon.

Despite the Spanish conquest, other countries fought to take over the Philippines. The Portuguese claimed their right to the islands because they actually lay on the Portuguese side of the pope's 1493 line of demarcation. After the Portuguese failed to take the islands, the Muslims invaded—but they also lost to the Spanish. Over the next few centuries, other colonization attempts were made by the English, Dutch, Chinese, and Japanese.

During the 1800s, Spain opened the islands to foreign trade and the archipelago's economy grew rapidly. Some Filipinos grew wealthy and sent their sons and daughters to universities in Manila and Europe. When they returned home, these educated young people began to seek political and social freedom from Spain.

A secret revolutionary society, the *Katipunan* (the Society of the Sons of the People) was formed in 1892 by Andres Bonifacio, an office clerk, to gain independence. Emilio Aguinaldo, a local chief of the Katipunan, was opposed to violence. He wanted to work for freedom through political reforms and a new government similar to that of the United States.

St. Lazarus Islands 1521; renamed Philippine Islands 1543

Luzon 1570
Manila
Colonized by Legazpi 1565
Guam 1521
Cebu
Brunei 1521
Riffins 1543
Tawi Tawi
Halmahera 1522
Equator
1526
1511

Spanish and Portuguese Possessions in 1580

Spanish possessions
Portuguese possessions

Fort Santiago

In 1592, Spanish conquerors under General Miguel Lopez de Legazpi began building a stone fortress at the mouth of the Pasig River on Luzon to defend against Moro invaders—Muslims from the southern Philippines. The fort helped defeat the Moros and discouraged others from attempting to take the islands. The fort was badly damaged in World War II, but today it is a national monument and a popular gathering place for lovers and artists.

Dr. José Rizal

Dr. José Rizal is a national martyr in the Philippines. Born in 1861, he was a physician, scientist, and writer who became an early crusader for Philippine independence from Spain. His speeches and novels helped develop Filipino nationalism. Although he led a nonviolent movement for independence, he was executed by a Spanish firing squad in 1896. His death convinced the people that there was no justice under Spanish rule. The mural shown here honors him.

After five years, the revolutionaries elected Aguinaldo as their president. Bonifacio was captured by Aguinaldo's supporters and executed. Fearing that the unrest would spread, the Spanish governor-general promised reforms if Aguinaldo ended the revolt and left the country. He agreed and sailed with his comrades to Hong Kong.

The Spanish-American War

The Spanish soon broke their promises to Aguinaldo, however. At the same time, freedom fighters in Cuba revolted, demanding their independence from Spain.

Sympathizing with the Cuban patriots, and also having colonial designs on Cuba, the United States sent the battleship USS *Maine* to protect American citizens in Cuba. The ship exploded in the harbor, and angry Americans blamed Spain.

The United States declared war on Spain on April 25,

1898. On May 1, in the first important battle of the brief Spanish-American War, the U.S. fleet under Admiral George Dewey destroyed all the Spanish ships in Manila Bay.

Two weeks later, Aguinaldo returned to the Philippines and led an army to help the Americans fight the Spaniards. On June 12, 1898, Aguinaldo declared the Philippines independent from Spain. One month before the first U.S. troops arrived, Aguinaldo's forces held all of provincial Luzon and laid siege to Manila.

In August, combined Filipino and American soldiers defeated the Spanish troops and the war ended. However, under a peace treaty signed with Spain in December, the United States gained possession of the Philippines and paid Spain $20 million for the islands.

War broke out again almost immediately, this time between the Philippines and the United States. Aguinaldo claimed that the American consul in Singapore had assured him of independence for the Philippines if it helped the United States in the war against Spain.

Fighting between Filipino and American soldiers began on February 4, 1899. All the major battles of the bloody Filipino-American War were fought on Luzon. Aguinaldo issued a Declaration of Independence on June 12, 1898, and the present Republic of the Philippines dates its independence from that declaration. Aguinaldo was captured in March 1901, but the fighting did not end until the following year. More than 200,000 Filipinos died in the war, either in battle or from disease.

Opposite: **Emilio Aguinaldo, commander of the Filipino revolutionaries**

American soldiers stand on a fort to declare U.S. rule in the Philippines.

The United States set up a colonial government in the Philippines in 1901 and promised self-rule was to come; not soon, but eventually. The first civilian governor was a U.S. federal judge, William Howard Taft, who later became president of the United States. To educate the Filipinos, the United States built schools in the Philippines and made education compulsory. Public health programs were established and the use of English was encouraged. U.S. businesses made large investments in the islands, and the Philippine economy soon became dependent on the United States.

Filipinos were allowed to serve in the government, and in 1935 the Philippines became a commonwealth with its own

President Manuel Quezon (waving) and his military adviser General Douglas MacArthur (right)

elected government and a Constitution modeled after that of the United States. Manuel Quezon was the first president of the Philippines Commonwealth. Local government had finally come to the Philippines, although the United States continued to make decisions for the new nation regarding foreign affairs and national defense.

Partly in exchange for economic aid from the United States, the Philippines government agreed to allow the United States to establish Clark Air Force Base and Subic Bay Naval Station on Luzon. These bases not only provided security for the Philippines against Communist expansion in the Pacific, but they also improved the country's economy because of military building and related industries. The United States withdrew its military bases from the Philippines in 1992.

Trade increased with other countries, and farmers began to use modern agricultural methods. However, stronger economic and military ties to the United States created a love-hate relationship between the two countries that would play itself out over the next decades.

Japanese Occupation in World War II

On December 7, 1941, Japanese planes bombed Pearl Harbor, the U.S. naval base in Hawaii, and attacked Clark Field, north of Manila. The United States declared war on Japan the next day and entered World War II. On December 10, Japanese troops disembarked from ships and invaded the Philippines. They reached Manila by January 2, 1942, and ransacked the city.

A U.S. military base on Corregidor Island that was bombed during the Pacific war

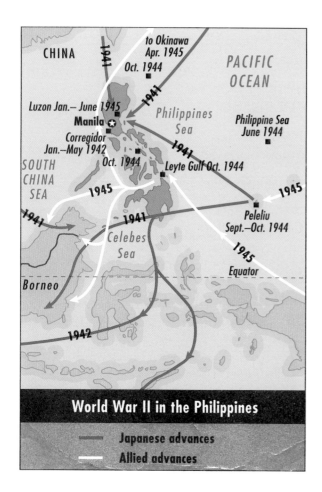

World War II in the Philippines

— Japanese advances
— Allied advances

Joint American and Filipino forces, led by U.S. general Douglas MacArthur, fought the Japanese until March 1942. The badly outnumbered Philippine–American forces were pushed onto Bataan Peninsula and into the dark, airless tunnels of Corregidor Island.

As the fighting turned in Japan's favor because it had more ships, planes, and troops in the Pacific, U.S. president Franklin D. Roosevelt ordered MacArthur to Australia so that the Allies could work up a plan to win the war in the Pacific.

At the urging of MacArthur, the Philippine's wartime president, Manuel Quezon, retreated to the United States with his wife and family, and members of his administration. Quezon set up a government-in-exile in Washington, D.C., but died less than a year later. His vice president, Sergio Osmena, succeeded him as president.

Douglas MacArthur

U.S. general Douglas MacArthur is a national hero to Filipinos. He served in the Philippines after graduation from West Point in 1903 and again in 1935, when he became head of the U.S. military mission to the new commonwealth of the Philippines.

After the Japanese attacked Hawaii and Manila in December 1941, MacArthur commanded the defense of the Philippines until March 1942. At that time, he left Corregidor to take command of Allied forces in the Southwest Pacific. After telling Filipinos "I shall return," he directed campaigns that led to the liberation of the Philippines. He made good his promise by returning to Leyte with an invasion force of 174,000 U.S. troops on October 20, 1944.

After MacArthur's departure from the Philippines, Lieutenant General Jonathan M. Wainwright took command of the U.S.–Filipino troops, but they were badly outnumbered. Wainwright ordered all Allied forces throughout the islands to lay down their weapons on June 9. Some 35,000 Philippine and American troops surrendered to the Japanese, and an additional 15,000 were captured. Many of them died on the Bataan "death march" to prison camps. The survivors starved. Many other Filipinos escaped to the mountains and continued fighting the Japanese until the end of the war.

In October 1944, MacArthur made a historic return to the Philippines leading a large new force. Philippine president Osmena accompanied MacArthur on his return to the Philippines. The battle to reclaim the islands from the Japanese lasted almost a year. Meanwhile, 120,000 Philippine civilians died in Manila due to Japanese atrocities.

A monument to General MacArthur's historic return to the Philippines, 1944

The destruction of the Japanese city of Nagasaki by the United States

In August 1945, the United States dropped atomic bombs on the Japanese cities of Hiroshima and Nagasaki to avoid a planned invasion of Japan that would have cost many more lives. The resulting devastation was so great that the Japanese surrendered on August 14, 1945, and signed a declaration on September 2 that ended the war in the Pacific.

Nearly 1 million Filipino people were killed or injured in the war, which also devastated the nation's economy. Manila suffered greater devastation during the war than any other capital except Warsaw, Poland. The entire city was almost destroyed by bombing, artillery, and grenades.

Independence at Last!

The United States granted the Philippines complete independence on July 4, 1946. The Republic of the Philippines was established with Manuel Roxas as president and Manila as the nation's capital. Roxas gained the presidency with the help of General MacArthur, who claimed Roxas had served bravely in the war as part of an underground Manila intelligence group.

Independence, however, did not bring political or economic stability to the nation. Even though U.S. aid to the country exceeded $2 billion, political unrest and poverty became widespread. After World War II, communists began infiltrating countries around the world, including the Philippines.

A communist-led group, the *Hukbong Magpapalayang Bayan* (People's Liberation Army), or Huks, operated out of the swamps and mountains of central Luzon where many of them had been guerrilla fighters during the war. Now their goal was to overthrow the new Philippine government. They sought to convert the Philippines to a communist form of government, dividing the estates of the wealthy landowners into small parcels of land that would be given to poor farmers. The Philippine army fought the Huks from 1949 until defeating them in 1954.

Manuel Roxas (left) and General MacArthur, 1946

Police surround a Huks operation in Manila.

Problems with Postwar Governments

President Roxas died of a heart attack in 1948 and was succeeded by his vice president, Elpidio Quirino, who was reelected the following year. Corruption and fraud during Quirino's presidency led to more economic decline.

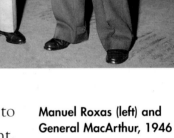

Ramon Magsaysay, a Philippine congressman and former secretary of national defense, became president in 1953 in an unusually honest election he won by a landslide. During his very successful presidency he reduced corruption and bureaucracy, and supported a responsible labor movement. His accidental death in a plane crash in 1957 was a tragedy, not only to the Philippines but to the rest of the world as well.

Carlos Garcia, Magsaysay's vice president, succeeded him as president. Because of corruption in his administration, he was not reelected but was succeeded by Diosdado Macapagal. Macapagal pushed an agricultural land-reform law through Congress. The law made tenant farmers leaseholders who would eventually own family-size farms. Macapagal was defeated in a bid for a second term in 1965 by Ferdinand Marcos, his former campaign manager.

The economy improved as Marcos encouraged foreign companies to build factories in the Philippines, and he was reelected in 1969. Meanwhile, communists renewed their efforts to infiltrate the government in the late 1960s and early 1970s.

Unity among groups of people in the Philippines began to unravel. Young Filipinos organized a New People's Army and attacked military installations. Moros, or Muslim Filipinos, demanded independence for parts of the islands with heavy Muslim populations.

President Marcos declared martial law in 1972. He virtually made war against groups in the provinces who opposed him, jailing many of his opponents. He controlled the news-

Ferdinand Marcos during his presidency

papers, radio, and television, abolished Congress, and gave police and the military powers to suppress unrest. In 1981, Marcos was reelected president for a six-year term.

U.S. president Ronald Reagan supported Marcos and encouraged generous economic aid despite warnings from his advisers that Marcos was misusing his power and funds from the United States that were intended to help the people. Marcos and his wife, Imelda, who was also governor of Metro Manila, lived a life of luxury in the presidential palace, isolated from the people and guarded by the military. Imelda Marcos became notorious for spending money on trifles such as a thousand pairs of shoes while many Filipinos went hungry.

Marcos's main political rival, Benigno S. Aquino Jr., was imprisoned for over seven years. In 1980, he was allowed to fly to the United States for heart surgery. He remained there for three years. Upon his return to the Philippines in 1983, he was shot to death at Manila's airport as he stepped off the plane. Marcos and his supporters were blamed for the murder.

Benigno S. Aquino Jr. defends himself before the Philippine Supreme Court after being sentenced to die by firing squad.

Opposition to President Marcos and his regime grew into what became known as the People Power Revolution. It resulted from the 1986 election in which Aquino's widow, Corazon "Cory" Aquino, opposed Marcos for the presidency. When she was forbidden to speak to the people at a rally in Manila, a half-million Filipinos protested, gathering in the streets, blocking traffic, and defying police. Many of them wore yellow T-shirts, headbands, armbands, and hats with slogans in support of Aquino.

Finally, Aquino was allowed to speak. She told the crowds, "Mister Marcos and his regime are truly evil and have systematically plundered our country and our people. Rarely has a nation been given an opportunity like this. It is certain our freedom will come. We have a chance to make history. I accept the challenge of the presidency."

Demonstrators rally against Marcos's declaration of martial law.

About 100 Filipinos were killed and many more injured by Marcos forces in preelection violence. Some 26 million people voted, more than 95 percent of those registered. Aquino won, but the National Assembly, largely controlled by Marcos, ruled that Marcos had won reelection. Tens of thousands of Filipinos throughout the provinces accused Marcos of stealing the election as well as countless millions of dollars from the people.

Public rebellion against Marcos continued for three angry and bloody weeks after the election. Then tens of thousands of Filipinos put their lives on the line at an anti-Marcos protest in Manila. Armed only with flowers, they linked arms and formed human barricades to face down Marcos's soldiers and tanks.

Nuns, priests, and seminarians in white cassocks in the front lines fell to their knees in front of the advancing military. Fingering rosary beads with one hand and touching the hot metal of the tanks with the other, they prayed aloud, "Hail Mary. . . ." The tanks halted and the soldiers stopped, unwilling to fire on their own people.

Virtual prisoners inside their palace in Manila, Marcos and his wife feared for their lives. President Reagan finally withdrew his support from Marcos but did not want further violence. The dictator, his family, and some of his supporters were airlifted out of the country by the U.S. Air Force. Ferdinand Marcos died in Hawaii in 1989, and Imelda Marcos was later convicted of illegally possessing U.S.$10 billion of the Philippine government's money, much of it foreign aid from the United States.

Filipinos show support for President Corazon Aquino at a rally for the new constitution.

President Aquino on a visit to Singapore

Corazon Aquino became president on February 25, 1986, and promised more democracy for the people of the Philippines. A new Constitution with many reforms was approved in February 1987. The Constitution provided for presidential terms of six years.

Aquino inherited serious economic problems from the Marcos years, including huge debts. The Philippines owed billions of dollars to foreign banks. Continuing political unrest prevented her from making her presidency more successful and democratic. She faced opposition from Marcos supporters; from the military, which objected to making deals with communist guerrillas; and from Filipinos who opposed the U.S. military presence and influence in the Philippines.

After several failed attempts by the military and communists to overthrow Aquino, a new election was held in 1992. According to law, she could not run for a second term, so she supported General Fidel V. Ramos, who was her defense minister and had been Marcos's deputy chief of staff of the armed forces. In a seven-way race that included Imelda Marcos, Ramos was elected president. Ramos improved the economy and distanced himself from the Marcos regime and policies. Joseph Estrada,

President Joseph Estrada (left) celebrates his sixty-second birthday.

Ramos's vice president, was elected president in 1998. Estrada was popular as a former action movie star and champion of the poor, but he was a supporter of the late dictator Ferdinand Marcos. In the 1998 election, fifty-one Filipinos were killed in election-related violence, although police said this was fewer than in past elections.

At the last minute, Imelda Marcos gave her support to Estrada, and the public chose him to lead them into the next century, even though some people wondered if justice would be served regarding the former first lady. Shortly after Estrada's election, his new government asked the Supreme Court to set aside a twelve-year prison sentence for Marcos and acquit her of corruption charges.

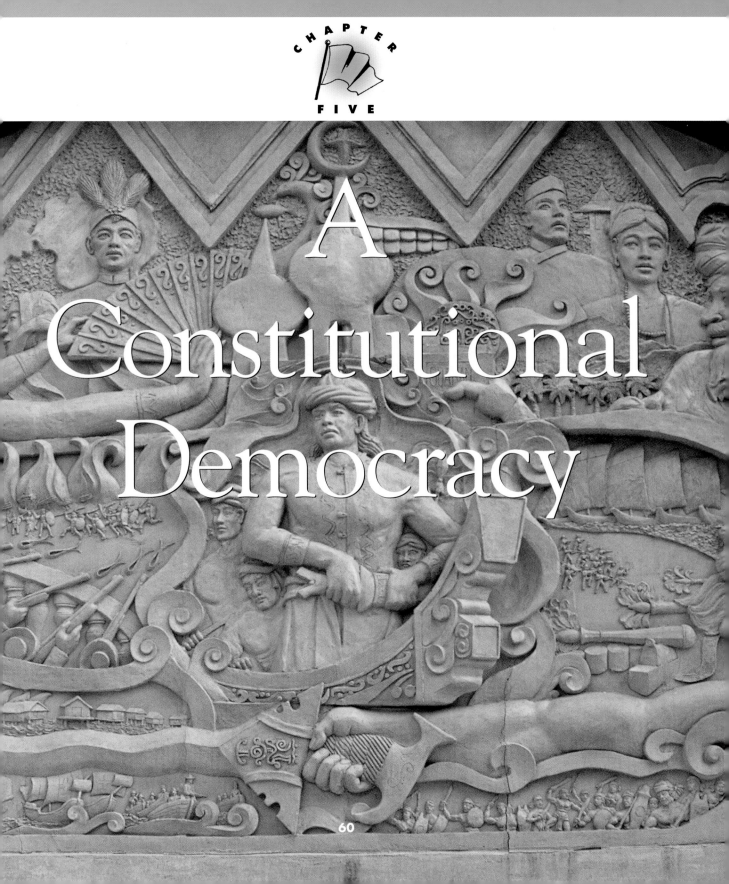

A Constitutional Democracy

A

FTER FOUR CENTURIES OF STRUGGLE FOR NATIONHOOD, the Republic of the Philippines celebrated its century mark as a nation in 1998. Centennial events marked Filipinos' pride in having the first constitutional democracy in Asia.

Opposite: **A tribute to the centennial of the freedom struggle, 1898–1998**

National Government

The Philippines has a constitutional form of government based upon a February 11, 1987, Constitution that is patterned largely on that of the United States. The 1987 Constitution replaced earlier constitutions that led to corruption and misuse of power. It sharply reduces the power of the president, which in the past sometimes led to tyranny in the Philippines. The president cannot make political appointments of friends or others who might let themselves be influenced, and also may not accumulate personal wealth while serving as president.

The capitol in Tacloban City, which is the capital of Leyte Province

To avoid dictatorships supported by the military, the Constitution also bars members of the military from holding political positions. It restores political freedoms and expands human rights guarantees that some previous presidents had taken away from the people. It calls for social justice based on substantial reforms in labor, land ownership, health, and housing, and it is considered the world's first constitution to contain the word *love*.

The Philippines is a republic whose government has three equal branches—the executive, the legislative, and the judiciary. They operate under a system of checks and balances according to the 1987 Constitution.

Malacanang Palace, the office and home of the president

The Executive Branch

The president is the head of state, aided by a vice president who also sits as a member of the president's cabinet. The president directs the executive branch of government and is limited to one six-year term. Presidents must be at least forty years old when elected. The vice president also serves a six-year term but may be reelected once, thus allowing him or her to serve for two consecutive terms.

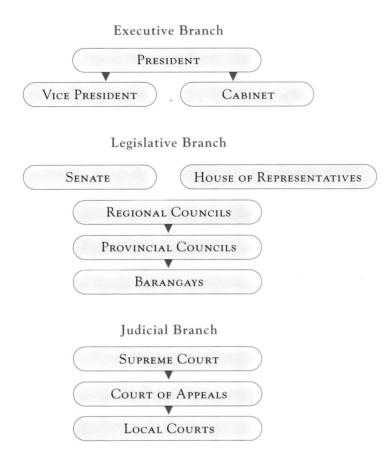

Executive Branch

PRESIDENT

VICE PRESIDENT   CABINET

Legislative Branch

SENATE   HOUSE OF REPRESENTATIVES

REGIONAL COUNCILS

PROVINCIAL COUNCILS

BARANGAYS

Judicial Branch

SUPREME COURT

COURT OF APPEALS

LOCAL COURTS

As chief executive, the president signs bills passed by the legislature and also acts as commander-in-chief of the nation's armed forces. The president names his or her cabinet members, but they must be approved by the legislature's Commission of Appointments.

The country's political system is similar to the U.S. system that inspired it, but it has several key differences. For one, in

the Philippines, the president and vice president are elected directly by popular vote. In the United States, a popular vote for president is overridden by an electoral college vote by state delegates. All Philippine citizens who are at least 18 years of age may vote.

Nuns voting in the national elections

The Legislative Branch

The Philippine Congress has a two-chamber structure similar to that of the United States, composed of the Senate, or upper house, with 24 senators, and the House of Representatives, or lower house, with a maximum of 254 representatives. Senators

The National Flag of the Philippines

The national flag of the Philippines, which came into use during the independence movement in 1898, consists of two horizontal bands. In peacetime, the top is blue and the bottom is red. In wartime, the colors are reversed. Blue stands for noble

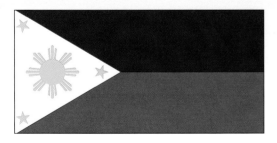

ideals and red for courage. The two colors are joined at the left side with a white triangle that represents the Filipino struggle against colonial Spain.

At the center of the white triangle is a yellow sun that stands for liberty. The sun's eight rays symbolize the eight provinces that first stood against Spanish occupation. In each of the three corners of the triangle is a yellow star representing the nation's three main regions—Luzon, the Visayan Islands, and Mindanao.

The Philippine National Anthem

"Filipinas," the national anthem of the Philippines, was a joint effort of a musician and a poet. On June 5, 1898, independence leader General Emilio Aguinaldo asked Julian Felipe, a Filipino pianist and composer, to compose a national march for the new country.

A week later, as Aguinaldo proclaimed the independence of the Philippines, Felipe's *Marcha Nacional Filipina* was played as the country's national flag was officially hoisted for the first time. The following year, a young Filipino poet, José Palma, wrote a poem, "Filipinas," which was filled with the revolutionary spirit of the period, and the poem was used as the words to the march. A Tagalog version by Felipe Padilla de Leon was officially adopted in 1935.

Land of the morning,
Child of the sun returning,
With fervor burning,
Thee do our souls adore.

Land dear and holy,
Cradle of noble heroes,
Ne'er shall invaders
Trample thy sacred shore.

Ever within thy skies and through thy clouds
And o'er thy hills and sea,
Do we behold the radiance, feel the throb,
Of glorious liberty.

Thy banner, dear to all our hearts,
Its sun and stars alight,
O Never shall its shining field
Be dimmed by tyrants' might!

Beautiful land of love,
O land of light,
In thine embrace 'tis rapture to lie,
But its glory ever, when thou art wronged,
for us, thy sons to suffer and die.

A Constitutional Democracy **65**

Filipinos line up at a high school in Manila to vote in the 1992 elections.

must be at least thirty-five years of age and native-born Filipinos. They are elected to six-year terms by the voters of the entire nation and may serve no more than two consecutive terms. They represent no particular district.

Voters from local districts elect 204 representatives to three-year terms. Up to 50 additional representatives are appointed by the president from lists drawn up by the political parties to ensure representation of women, ethnic minorities, and certain economic and labor groups. Representatives must be at least twenty-five years of age and native-born Filipinos. They can serve only three terms in a row.

The Judicial Branch

The Supreme Court is the highest court in the Philippines. It consists of a chief justice and fourteen associate justices, each appointed by the president for terms of four years. The president also appoints all other judges in the country.

The Court of Appeals, which reviews decisions made by lower courts, consists of a presiding justice and fifty associate justices. Each Philippine city has its own court. Each municipality has a judge who serves at the local court.

Local Government

The Philippine national government was once highly centralized and bound with bureaucracy and red tape. Since the adoption of the Local Government Code in 1987, more functions have been given to local government units.

The country is divided into thirteen regions plus the National Capital Region (Metro Manila) and the Autonomous Regions, each governed by a regional council. The regions are further divided into more than seventy provinces, each with a governor, a vice governor, and two provincial board members. They are elected by the people and serve four-year terms.

Each province consists of a provincial capital city and several municipalities (towns). Elected mayors and councils govern the Philippines' cities and municipalities. The municipalities in turn are composed of village communities called *barangays*. These are the smallest sociopolitical administration units in the nation. The term *barangay* comes from the name of the large oceangoing outrigger boats used by Malays to migrate to the Philippines many years ago. Each of the nation's 42,000 barangays has a captain, six councilmen, a treasurer, and a secretary. Every citizen is a member of a barangay assembly that meets to discuss national and local issues.

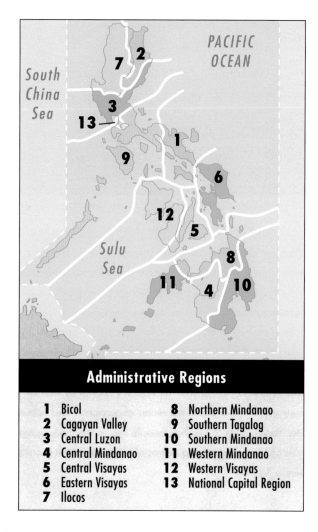

Administrative Regions

1	Bicol	8	Northern Mindanao
2	Cagayan Valley	9	Southern Tagalog
3	Central Luzon	10	Southern Mindanao
4	Central Mindanao	11	Western Mindanao
5	Central Visayas	12	Western Visayas
6	Eastern Visayas	13	National Capital Region
7	Ilocos		

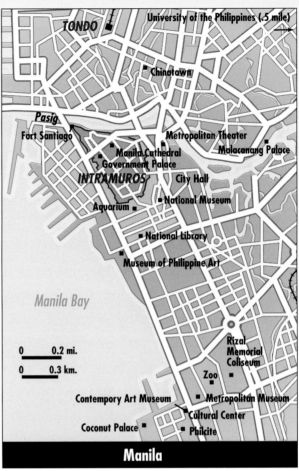

Manila

Manila: Did You Know This?

The Spanish called Manila the "Noble and Ever Loyal City," meaning the people were faithful to the Malay tradition of friendliness. This is still true of the very cosmopolitan city of Manila today.

The city began as a walled fort erected by Spanish conquerors in 1571. It grew from a dozen small cities and towns that clustered along Manila Bay, one of the world's finest harbors, to become the nation's capital as well as its most important city and the center of economic and cultural life. Today, over 12 million people live in the 146-square-mile (378-sq-km) Manila metropolitan area, which is called Metro Manila.

Politically Active Citizens

Filipinos have had their independence only since the late 1940s, but they have already experienced great dissatisfaction with some of their elected leaders. Perhaps because their presidents and other politicians sometimes took away their rights and plundered the nation's treasury, most Filipinos are active in local and national politics. The younger generation of voters actively condemn so-called traditional politics ruled by "goons, guns, and gold."

There are often up to a dozen political parties in the Philippines. Each party has its own leading candidates for office who may have conflicting agendas tied to their own special interests. The two main political parties are Laban Ng Masang Pilipino (LAMP) and Lakas Ng Bayan (Lakas/NUCD).

The idea of democracy is strong among Filipinos, but the institutions of democracy in the country are sometimes not as strong. This has led to Filipinos being influenced by family, cultural, ethnic, and other political traditions. In the past, these varied influences have encouraged some politicians to divide the people, to cheat and lie, and to steal from the treasury. A more educated middle class may reject the previous political traditions that so often led to dictatorship and graft.

A U.S. naval base in Olangapo, 1990

Philippine–U.S. Relations

"Relations between the Philippines and the United States are based on shared history and commitment to democratic principles, as well as on vibrant economic ties," according to a 1998 statement from the U.S. State Department Bureau of East Asian and Pacific Affairs. "The historical and cultural links between our countries remain strong.

"The Philippines modeled its governmental institutions on those of the U.S., and continues to share a commitment to democracy and human rights. At the most fundamental level of bilateral relations, human links continue to form a strong bridge between us. There are about 2 million Americans of Philippine ancestry in the United States and more than 100,000 American citizens in the Philippines."

A Country of
Varied Wealth

O NCE DEPENDENT UPON AGRICULTURE, THE PHILIPPINE economy is now stronger and more diversified because manufacturing has taken the lead in production value. In 1998, about 39.8 percent of Filipinos worked in farming, forestry, or fishing. Another 43.7 percent had jobs in service industries such as government, education, medicine, trade, tourism, transportation, communication, and banking. The rest worked in manufacturing, construction, and mining, and in other industries.

Opposite: **Ifugao rice terraces**

Water buffalo are used to plow the rice paddies.

Agriculture

Although only about 35 percent of the nation's land is farmed, Filipinos produce most of their own food. Rice and corn grow on about two-thirds of the archipelago's cultivated land. Other leading food crops are sweet potatoes and cassava, a starchy root.

Many Filipinos do not own their own land but rent the land they farm and pay the owner a share of the crop. Most farms are on the lowlands, but crops are also raised on hillsides and mountain slopes.

A sugarcane train

Bananas, pineapples, coconuts, mangoes, and sugarcane are grown for both local use and export. Farmers also raise hogs, poultry, and tobacco. Many rural families raise chickens and gather the eggs for family use and for sale at local markets.

The Philippines' major export commodity is sugar. Sugarcane fields are located on other islands but the Visayan island of Negros produces 61 percent of the nation's sugar.

Coconut products are the third most important export of the Philippines, surpassed only by sugar and semiconductor

What the Philippines Grows, Makes, and Mines

Agriculture (1996)

Sugarcane	26,000,000 metric tons
Rice	11,283,570 metric tons
Coconuts	10,000,000 metric tons

Manufacturing (1995; value added in Philippine pesos)

Food products	176,200,000,000
Petroleum and coal products	36,900,000,000
Chemicals	35,700,000,000

Mining (1996)

Coal	1,047,336 metric tons
Nickel ore	378,921 metric tons
Copper concentrate	188,442 metric tons

technology devices. The islands produce 20 percent of the world's coconuts and the products derived from them, such as copra, shredded coconut, and coconut oil. The oil is used in many parts of the world to make margarine, soap, detergents, plastics, candy bars, and cake frostings. The Philippines is a major supplier of coconut oil to the United States.

Coconut trees grow to a height of 100 feet (30 m), and a single tree may produce as many as 200 coconuts a year. The average is about 30 nuts. While coconut trees are found on many islands in the archipelago, most are grown on small farms throughout the islands or raised on plantations on Luzon, Mindanao, and on the Visayan islands of Cebu, Leyte, Samar, and Albay.

About half of the Philippine banana crop is exported. Large banana freighters with refrigerated holds can be seen in Davao Gulf. Japan imports most of the banana crop sold to foreign markets.

One-third of the archipelago's pineapples, fresh and canned, are consumed on the islands. The remaining harvest is shipped to other countries. Pineapple canning is one of the few

The Sugar King

Victor Gaston, once called the "Sugar King" of the Philippines, is credited with making the Philippines a world leader in the production and marketing of sugar in the early 1900s. He managed and improved a sugar mill on Negros that was founded by his father, Yves Gaston, a Frenchman. The colonial mansion Victor Gaston lived in with his wife and twelve children until his death in 1927 is open to the public in Silay City, Negros Occidental. It is now called Balay Negrense Museum.

Pineapple canning is an important food-processing industry.

large-scale food-processing industries of the Philippines, along with sugar and coconuts. Two-thirds of the pineapple exports are canned. Other fruits that grow on the islands include papayas, cassavas, and melons, which are sold at open-air markets.

Coffee plantations are located above the 1,000-foot (305-m) level in the uplands of Batangas Province of Luzon, south of Manila Bay, and on the mountainsides of Mindanao. Cacao, from which chocolate is produced, grows in the same regions.

Fish are laid out to dry after they are caught.

Fishing Industry

Filipinos catch anchovies, mackerel, sardines, tuna, and other fish in the surrounding waters. Crab and shrimp are found in the lakes. Shrimp, milkfish, and tilapia are raised in ponds along the coast and near river mouths.

The most productive fishing grounds are the coastal waters, where mangrove swamps along the shores and coral reefs bring nutrients to the waters. About fifty-two large fishing grounds are the province of commercial fishers.

About 15 percent of the marine fish production occurs in the coral reefs. Coral is collected for construction and ornaments, but since about half of the coral reefs have been overused, a ban was placed on exporting and trading coral.

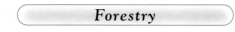
Even after years of severe deforestation, the Philippine forests are the most diversified in Southeast Asia. The government owns most of the forests. Large commercial forests are found on Mindanao, Palawan, and Luzon.

The export of Philippine lumber to Japan and the United States has declined since the depletion of the forests that cover two-thirds of the country. However, more than 3,000 kinds of trees still grow on the islands.

About 90 percent of the nation's lumber comes from Philippine mahogany trees, though other trees such as mangroves and pines also yield wood. The kapok tree produces a fiber used in insulation, mattresses, and upholstery. Bamboo grows throughout the islands, and its thick, hollow stems are used in building houses and making baskets, furniture, and other items.

Destruction of Philippine rain forests to supply wood for the world market has had severe repercussions. Both the wildlife that inhabited the forests and the people who lived there and depended on the forestland for food and shelter have been affected.

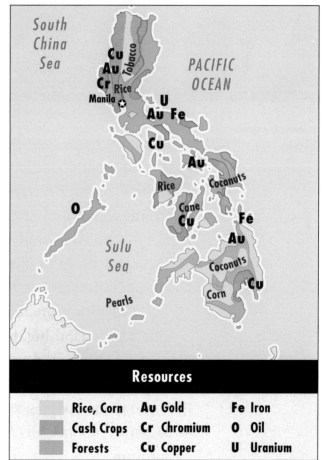

Resources

Rice, Corn	Au Gold	Fe Iron
Cash Crops	Cr Chromium	O Oil
Forests	Cu Copper	U Uranium

Strip-mining for gold and copper

Mining and Manufacturing

The Philippines are rich in minerals that make up a large part of the country's exports. Copper, the leading mineral, is mainly found on Luzon, Cebu, Negros, and Samar. Northern Luzon has large gold mines. Other minerals on the islands include deposits of chromite, coal, iron ore, limestone, manganese, silver, nickel, and zinc.

Philippine manufacturing plants produce cement, chemicals, cigars, clothing, foods and beverages, refined metals and petroleum, sugar, textiles, and wood products. Many factories operate in special export-processing zones where owners can import foreign goods without paying import taxes. These factories produce electronic equipment, clothing, shoes, and furniture.

The Philippines, like most island countries, cannot produce everything its people need, so foreign trade, mostly with the United States and Japan, is important. The chief imports to the Philippines are chemicals, machinery, and petroleum. The main exports are electronic equipment and clothing. The country also exports bananas, coconut products, copper, gold, lumber, pineapples, sugar, orchids, asparagus, and prawns. Manila is the country's most important port for both domestic and international trade.

Philippine political stability has resulted in increased U.S. investment in the country, while a strong security relationship rests on the U.S.-Philippines Mutual Defense Treaty (August 30, 1951). This treaty provides that the countries will protect each other against any external armed attack. The United States has traditionally been the Philippines' largest trading partner, taking about 44 percent of Philippine exports and providing about 25 percent of its imports in 1997. Two-way trade with the United States in 1997 was more than U.S. $17.8 billion.

Filipinos manufacturing products for export

Principal U.S. exports to the Philippines include materials for semiconductor, electronic, and electrical machinery manufacture; electric and nonelectric machinery; transport equipment; and cereals. Major Philippine exports to the U.S. are textiles

Philippine Currency

The currency in the Philippines is the peso (P), which is broken into 100 centavos. Centavo coin are available in 1, 5, 25, and 50 denominations, similar to the penny, nickel, quarter, and fifty-cent pieces used in the United States. Filipinos also have 1-, 2-, and 5-peso coins. Paper currency is printed in denominations of 5, 10, 20, 50, 100, and 500 pesos. In 1999, U.S.$1 was equal to 39.3 pesos.

The paper currency pictures historically important Filipinos and various symbols. P20 notes, for instance, feature the image of former Philippine president Manuel L. Quezon on the front. *Saligang Batas* 1935 represents the ratification of the 1935 Constitution. *Wikang Pambansa* marks the adoption of Pilipino as the country's national language. There is also the logo of the Commonwealth Government, the form of government during the term of President Quezon. On the back of the P20 bill is a picture of Malacanang Palace, the official office and home of the current Philippine president.

and garments, electric machinery, semiconductor devices, and coconut oil. U.S. investment in the Philippines continues to be extensive, estimated at more than U.S.$2 billion, making the United States the largest foreign investor in the Philippines.

A Vacation Paradise

The Philippines is very popular with tourists because of the archipelago's natural beauty and the Filipinos' friendliness and hospitality. The islands' beaches and water recreation areas as well as its refreshing mountain resorts attract visitors from all over the world throughout the year.

Markets are popular places to shop.

Cost of Living

Many things are a lot less expensive in the Philippines than in the United States and Canada. With 1 peso, you can buy two small chocolate bars, and 5 pesos buys a small bottle of soda. A typical rock-concert ticket ranges from P100 (U.S.$2.50) to P1,000 (U.S.$25). A music compact disc costs P300 (U.S.$7.50) to P500 (U.S.$12.50). A movie ticket costs P50 (U.S.$1.25) to P60 (U.S.$1.50).

It may seem as if Filipinos pay less for these things than Americans or Canadians do in their countries, but the Philippine peso is valued differently. Many Filipinos earn the equivalent of only U.S.$4 or U.S.$5 a day, so it would take them more than a day to earn enough to buy a compact disc.

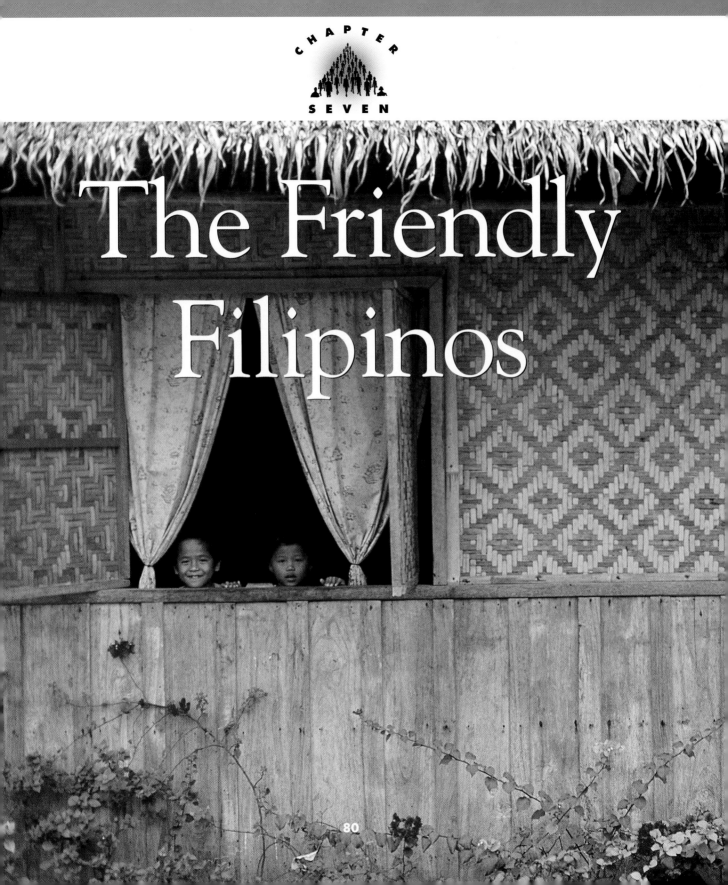

The Friendly Filipinos

M ANY PEOPLE SAY THE BEST THING THE PHILIPPINES EXPORTS is friendliness. Otherwise, most foreigners would have a hard time describing a "typical" Filipino. That's because there is no "typical" Filipino, except in the broadest generalizations.

The people may be best categorized by their cultural heritage, which reflects racial or religious differences. More than 90 percent are Christians, living mainly as farmers and fishers in the lowlands or as professionals and workers in the cities. While farmers and fishers are numerous in the lowland rural areas, many professionals, such as teachers, also live in small towns throughout the provinces.

The Tagalogs live in central and southern Luzon, especially in Manila, the capital city. Visayan groups dominate the central Philippines, while a mixture of Luzon and Visayan migrants make up the Christian settlements in Mindanao.

Muslim Filipinos, also called Moros, live in southern Mindanao and the Sulu islands. Tausugs and Samals live by the sea, while Magindanaos and Maranaos live in the hills and mountains. The

Opposite: **Filipino boys look out a window in Bohol.**

Muslims socialize outside a mosque.

Who Lives in the Philippines?

Christian Malay	91.5%
Muslim Malay	4%
Chinese	1.5%
Other	3%

Moros, a very independent people, strongly resisted colonization by the Spanish and the Americans. They were, however, helpful to American soldiers who were lost in the jungle during World War II.

The rest of the Filipinos live in the more remote parts of the country. These include natives of the Cordilleras, shy Aytas in the mountains, Mindanao hill tribes who wear colorful costumes, and the gentle Mangyans of Mindoro.

In 1971, a remote tribe called the Tasaday was discovered living in the dense Mindanao rain forests. Previously unknown to the world, they became the subject of worldwide amazement because they lived in caves and used the simple stone tools of a Stone Age people. The government set aside a protected area of land for them on Mindanao.

At the other extreme, Filipinos in Manila and other cities of the archipelago live and work as people do in most cities of the world today. They enjoy the modern conveniences and luxuries and suffer the noise, congestion, and pollution that go with them.

Although Filipinos are of predominantly Malay ancestry, they have the marks of several other races in their cul-

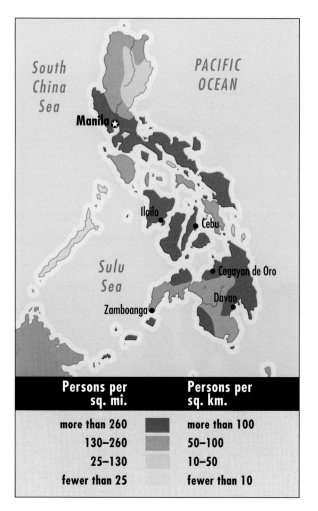

Persons per sq. mi.		Persons per sq. km.
more than 260		more than 100
130–260		50–100
25–130		10–50
fewer than 25		fewer than 10

ture, if not actually in their blood. The archipelago was a Spanish colony for three centuries, then an American colony for more than four decades, from 1898 to 1946. Add to that their centuries of interaction with the Chinese and various Muslim Asians as well as the islands' own regional native differences.

Minority groups may differ in physical appearance and have their own language and culture, but it is primarily clothing and artifacts that distinguish individuals. Once they are educated or urbanized, hill people are racially indistinguishable from most other Filipinos.

The largest minority group—the Visayans—lives on the sugar-rich central islands. In Luzon, the Tagalogs, from the provinces near Manila, are considered to be the most home-loving Filipinos. The Ilocanos, from the north, are said to be the most energetic and thrifty, while the Pampanguenos from the central plains are considered the sharpest in trading. The Muslims in the far southern islands are seen as the most independent.

A Batak tribeswoman and her child

Most minority groups live in the mountains, while others live along rivers or shallow seas. Their lives are continually changing as roads are built into their remote communities and they are linked to the rest of the world by radio, television, and satellite dishes. They then become more absorbed into the mainstream of the country. Most young people welcome these changes and prefer to learn the new ways rather than keep to the old traditions.

There are at least sixty ethnic groups in the Philippines. They are distributed mainly around northern Luzon, where the groups include the Bontoc, Ibaloi, Ifugao, Ilocano, Kalinga, and Tingguian. Central Luzon has the Negrito, Mindoro has the Mangyan, and western Mindanao and the Sulu Islands

An Ifugao couple

have the Muslims. Members of cultural minorities are often descended from the archipelago's early settlers. They follow their own rich traditions in crafts, clothes, music, language, and religion.

An Ayta man

Aytas (Negritos)

Many cultural groups in the Philippines are the descendants of early settlers who came by sea, but the Aytas—also called Negritos—traveled overland from Borneo many thousands of years ago, before the end of the Ice Age. They eventually fled to the mountains and the remote coastal foothills to escape Spanish rule or conversion to Islam or Christianity.

The descendants of these Aytas live throughout the islands today but mainly in the Cordillera Central of Luzon, Mindoro, Palawan, and Mindanao. Short and dark-skinned with tightly curled hair, they speak Malay-Polynesian languages. They seldom marry outside their cultural group, so they retain their bloodlines and folk ways. Although some are Christian, they also maintain their ancient lifestyles.

Ethnic Chinese

Chinese traders arrived in the Philippines even before the Spaniards. By 1600, there were more than 30,000 Chinese living in the archipelago. They were helpful as intermediaries in trade between the Spanish and the natives, and they were also skilled craftspeople and artisans. Their descendants enjoy major economic, social, and political positions in the Philippines today.

Filipino Culture

Sociologists agree on some generally accepted Filipino traits and values. Close family ties go beyond parents, brothers and sisters, aunts and uncles, cousins, and grandparents. Family love, loyalty, and respect extend to entire clans. The clans are led by *compadres* (godfathers) and *comadres* (godmothers). And compadres and comadres may not even be blood relatives, but community leaders. They sponsor couples at their weddings, and then the babies that follow. They become like part of the family.

Loyalty is owed first to one's family, then to compadres, friends, schoolmates, and neighbors. Gratitude is another side of Filipino loyalty. Even a small favor is paid back and never forgotten. If a local politician does a family a favor, the entire clan will show its gratitude by voting for him or her, again and again.

Several Tagalog terms describe Filipino cultural traits, such as *bahala na,* a casual "what happens, happens" attitude. While Filipinos work hard to get ahead, they also believe that what happens is in the hands of God. *Pakikisama* is a deep

Opposite: **A local family of Siargao Island**

A Filipina in native costume

camaraderie and helpfulness, even with strangers. *Utang na loob* refers to the value placed on tit-for-tat (you give to me, I give back to you) settlement of debts of gratitude.

To most of the world, Filipinos have earned a positive image for several things: being friendly and peace-loving yet ready to fight for their rights or to correct an injustice. They proved this bravely in World War II and in the Vietnam and Korean Wars, and more recently in the 1986 revolution when they toppled the oppressive regime of President Ferdinand Marcos. They are also considered honest and hardworking, with a willingness to cooperate for mutual gain or benefit. This is shown by the millions of immigrants and contract workers living in the United States, Canada, and other countries who send money home to help support family members on the islands.

Language

The official language of the Philippines is Pilipino, based mainly on Tagalog. The Pilipino language was created by the government in 1937 to unify the country. English is used in government, big business, and higher education. The Philippines is the world's third-largest English-speaking country, but most Filipinos speak several languages, unlike most Americans. Although many of the more than sixty ethnic groups have their own language, eight major dialects are spoken by about 90 percent of the people.

Most Filipinos speak Pilipino as a second language, after either English or their ethnic or minority language. Many Pilipino words, such as *barrio*, *compadre*, and *fiesta*, come from Spanish. Tagalog, used mainly in Manila and central Luzon, is the language of about 25 percent of homes.

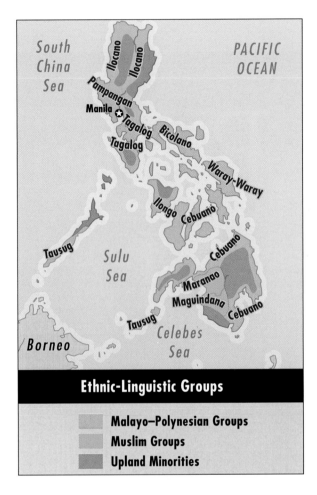

Ethnic-Linguistic Groups

- Malayo–Polynesian Groups
- Muslim Groups
- Upland Minorities

Common Pilipino Words and Phrases

Magandang umaga po (ma-gahn-DAHNG oo-MA-go PO)	Good morning
Magandang hapon po (ma-gahn-DAHNG HA-pone PO)	Good afternoon
Magandang gabi po (ma-gahn-DAHNG GAHBI)	Good evening
oo (oh-oh)	yes
hindi/hindi po (HIN-dee/HIN-dee PO)	no
Salamat po (sa-LA-maht po)	Thank-you
mabuhay (ma-boo-Hi)	welcome *or* farewell

Religion and Mythology

FILIPINOS ARE VERY RELIGIOUS PEOPLE, and their faith plays an important part in their daily lives. The Philippines is the only predominantly Christian country in Asia. The religious beliefs of many people include their cultural heritage, which is a blend of Western and Eastern philosophies and rituals.

Besides the established religion they practice, many Filipinos also believe in a universal god called Bathala who rules the earth and the universe and decides their fate. Even many Christian Filipinos take part in ancient rituals and pray to the rain god during a drought, for example, or to the earth god for a bountiful harvest. Often, they pray to the gods through a local spokeswoman, the *diwatero*, who is a healer or spirit medium. Some people worship animals, trees, and rocks. Many Filipinos also worship their ancestors—called *anitos*—and pray to them for guidance and protection.

The interior of Saint James Church

Opposite: **A mosque in Zamboanga**

Major Religions of the Philippines

Roman Catholic	83%
Protestant	9%
Muslim	5%
Buddhist and other faiths	3%

The Spanish Bring Christianity

Roman Catholicism came to the Philippines through priests from a series of missionary orders. In 1565, Augustinian friars accompanied conquistador Miguel Lopez de Legazpi to the archipelago. They were followed by the Franciscans, and then the Jesuits and the Dominicans. The missionaries not only brought Christianity to the natives and had churches built but also introduced Western culture, hospitals, schools, and universities.

Most Filipinos, however, did not totally accept the Westernized Christianity of the missionaries. They insisted upon keeping many of their folk traditions and rituals, which even today make the Filipino form of Christianity unique.

Protestant missionaries came to the Philippines during the period of U.S. colonization in the early 1900s. Today, small congregations of Episcopalians, Baptists, Lutherans, Methodists, and Presbyterians worship on the principal islands, where they have their own churches, schools, and health clinics. The Filipino Independent Church (*Aglipayan*) was founded in 1890 by Gregorio Aglipay as a nationalist Catholic church for Filipinos.

Both Catholic and Protestant Filipinos worship the Virgin Mary and the Child Jesus and pray to them at home altars. Prayers may be for good health, protection while traveling, or a rich harvest.

Christian rituals such as baptism, confirmation, and first communion are major

Religious Holidays

Filipinos celebrate five Christian religious events nationwide each year:

Holy Thursday	March/April
Good Friday	March/April
Easter Sunday	March/April
All Saints Day	November 1
Christmas Day	December 25

events in the lives of most Catholic Filipinos, strengthening the entire family's faith. In the church's marriage ceremony, a young person completes his or her transition to responsible adulthood. The final ritual is performed when a dying person receives Holy Communion for the last time.

Daily Christian rituals include morning mass, prayer before meals, and family rosaries. Special religious events include visiting several churches on Holy Thursday during Lent, the blessing of fire and wood on Black Saturday, midnight mass on Christmas Eve, and offering flowers to the Virgin Mary in May. Priests or ministers are often asked to bless a new car before it is used, a new house before it is occupied, or a new flower shop or restaurant before it is opened to the public.

Christian churches are often the most important buildings in a town, and the priest or minister is an important person in the community. Each town holds its annual fiesta in honor of its patron saint. On these holy occasions, many folk influences are added to the Christian traditions, especially during Holy Week before and during Easter, and at Christmas.

A girl during her first Holy Communion ceremony

A reenactment of Jesus' procession to the crucifixion site during an Easter festival

Some of the most devout holy events occur on Good Friday. In Maranduque and in the town of San Fernando, on the Pampanga, some men have their backs whipped or even allow themselves to be nailed to a cross. Church officials do not encourage such fanaticism, but the traditions are deep among many Filipinos and they will not give them up.

Early Filipinos believed in the soul and in life after death even before Christianity arrived on the islands and reinforced their beliefs. Some Filipinos today add their own religious folk traditions such as belief in fairies, elves, hexes and spells, and ghosts.

Islam

Islamic missionaries from Arabia and elsewhere came to the Philippines in the late 1300s, a few decades before the first Christian missionaries arrived. The Muslims' religious influence among natives in the southern islands was so strong that they could not later be converted to Christianity.

Filipino Muslims are part of the Sunni sect, which has a worldwide majority. Formal doctrine from the Koran—the Muslim holy book—and the faith of Islam are often blended with Filipino animistic worship of animals, natural objects, and spirits, as they are by Christian Filipinos.

Muslims, the largest of the minority religious groups, live mainly on the island of Mindanao and the Sulu Archipelago. Of the many Muslim groups, each with its own culture and language, the three main ones are the Tausug, the Maranao, and the Magindanao.

Muslims celebrating Eid el Fitr, the end of the fast of Ramadan, at a mosque

Other Religions

Many other Filipinos with strong ties to their traditional beliefs fled to the mountains to escape being converted to Christianity or Islam. Today, their descendants—the Aytas—and other highland tribes are animists. Animists

believe that all natural objects, both living and nonliving—such as streams, trees, wind, and rocks—have a spirit, or life force.

Opposite: **A Chinese Taoist temple in Cebu City**

The Chinese communities have a small number of Buddhists and Taoists. Taoism, however, is considered a moral and political philosophy rather than a religion. A small minority of Hindus and Sikhs have their own places of worship.

Faith Healing and Herb Doctors

A Filipino's faith is often a blend of traditional religion and ancient Philippine customs and mythology. For example, many Filipinos are strong believers in faith healing—curing an illness by prayer or touch and incantation, without medical instruments or drugs.

Most of the Philippines' estimated 15,000 faith healers and herb doctors are devout Christians. About 80 of them claim to be "psychic surgeons." Many belong to a union—the

Good Luck Charm

Many less-educated, provincial Filipinos believe that wearing an amulet called *anting-anting* around their neck will ward off evil and bring good health or good luck. The good luck talisman is often a combination of Christian and folk elements. It may be worn around the neck and bear the image of a saint and the words of a prayer. A folk amulet may be kept at home along with symbols of good health or good luck such as a crocodile's tooth, tree bark, or pig's hair.

Filipino history tells of peasants without weapons who armed themselves with anting-anting and rushed against their enemies. They were convinced bullets would not harm them, but, unfortunately, they were killed.

Christian Spiritists Union of the Philippines—which believes the gift of healing should be given freely to those in need.

Instead of calling a licensed medical doctor if someone is ill, a faith healer or an herb doctor may be called. The most simple form of faith healing is praying that the illness will heal itself. Some healers lay hands on the afflicted part of the sick person's body or apply herbs or oils while chanting to make the illness go away. Others claim to cure the illness by putting the sick person in a trance. The practice is especially used by the poor because many faith healers in the Philippines believe if they ask a fee, they may lose their power.

Black Saturday

Filipino religious mythology is perhaps strongest on Black Saturday, the day before Easter Sunday. It is believed that extraordinary powers can be acquired if, at midnight on Black Saturday, a believer finds a banana blossom about to open. As it opens, the blossom ejects a tearlike dewdrop called *mutya*. If you catch the dewdrop in your mouth you will battle with evil spirits until dawn. If you can endure the struggle until Easter morning, you will acquire supernatural powers that ward off evil, ill health, and bad fortune.

How Things Came to Be

Elders in many ancient Filipino tribes created legends to teach the young the origin of the natural world around them and tell them how they should behave and how good can overcome evil. An ancient tale, for instance, tells how the first Filipino came to be. God made the first person like a cookie, but baked it too long and it came out black. God tried again, but this time didn't bake the person long enough and it came out white. The third time God baked the cookie, it came out brown, beautiful, and just right—like the Filipino.

In a northern Luzon legend, the sky was once low, but a maiden pounded her rice so hard that the wooden pole she pounded with pushed up the sky. Jewelry she hung on the clouds became the stars that shine at night.

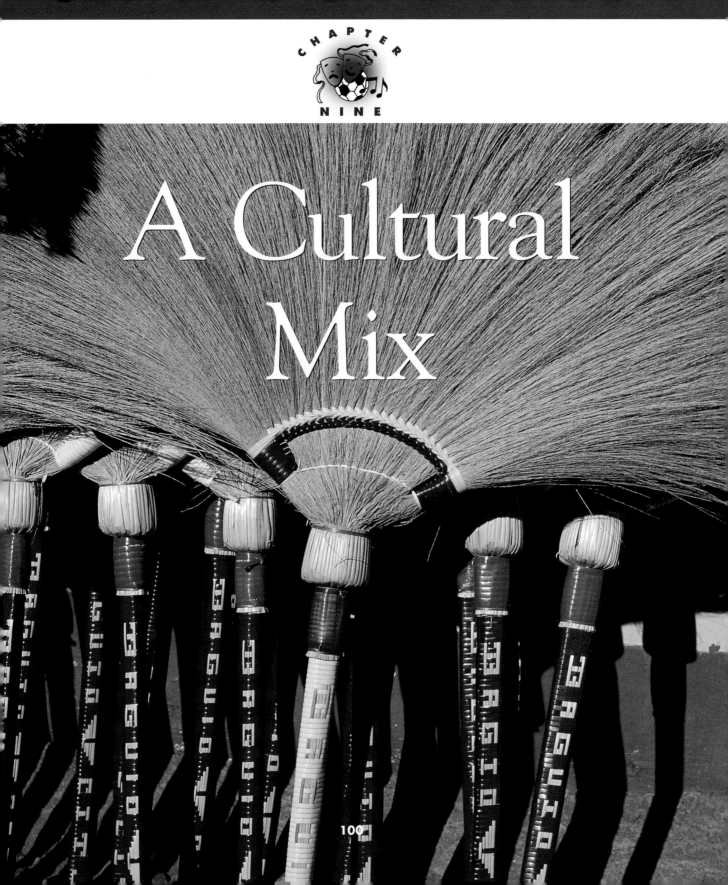

A Cultural
Mix

CULTURAL LIFE IN THE PHILIPPINES REFLECTS THE NATION'S blending of Asian and Western influences together with the islands' own folklore and traditions. Art, architecture, and dance ranges from the primitive to the very modern.

Opposite: **Native brooms**

Art in the Philippines

Philippine art is often characterized by Spanish and folk traditions or other Western influences. When the Filipino Academy of Painting was established in 1821, it was dominated by Spanish themes and techniques. The first internationally recognized Filipino painters, Juan Luna and Felix Resurreccion Hidalgo, won prizes in 1884 at the Madrid Exposition in Spain. Over the years, Filipino painters have largely turned away from

A mural in Rizal Park, Manila

The Cultural Center of the Philippines

What the Lincoln Center for the Performing Arts in New York is to Americans, the Cultural Center of the Philippines in Manila is to Filipinos. It is the center of the nation's visual and performing arts, with seven theaters and six resident companies for music, dance, and drama.

The Main Theater, where concerts are held and dramas are staged, features an abstract-mural curtain designed by Galo Ocampo, a master Filipino painter. The Little Theater presents chamber music and native or foreign plays in Pilipino. The Folk Arts Theater is the stage for Filipino and international pop stars. New books are launched at the Coconut Place, built with materials from coconut trees.

works depicting social or historic themes. They express their own ideas in works exhibited in many galleries and at the Museum of Philippine Contemporary Art in Manila.

The Museum of Philippine Ethnographic Art exhibits life-size tableaux highlighting Filipino arts and crafts. The Contemporary Art Museum of the Philippines features seasonal shows of paintings and sculpture by major Filipino artists.

Crafts of the Philippines

Filipinos are skilled at many traditional arts and crafts of great diversity and intricate beauty. They are excellent basket weavers and their products come in all sizes, shapes, and designs. The craft is an art form among the mountain tribes of Mindanao, Mindoro, and Palawan.

Another domestic art is textile weaving. Fabrics include *pina* and *jusi*, woven from pineapple and banana fibers. These finely embroidered, translucent cloths rival French and Belgian lace. The T'boli people dye tree bark and weave the strands into geometric designs for baskets and

Mindayan textile weaving

mats. Yakans weave bright colors into their mats and clothing.

Wood carvings of animals, birds, and other objects, and wood furniture-making are important native arts. Moros carve marvelous wooden grave markers and houses. In the town of Paete, on Laguna, wood-carving is the community's only industry. Some of the Philippines' finest furniture is carved in the town of Betis, on Pampanga. Other handicrafts are the shell craft of Cebu and the silver filigree of Baguio.

A wood-carver at work

Drama

Philippine drama originally focused on tribal themes and activities, and later drew upon ideas of nationalism and independence. Today, plays reflecting Philippine history, religious events, and daily life are performed in both Pilipino and English. Foreign classics, such as Shakespeare's plays, are performed mainly in university theaters. Contemporary Western stage plays and musicals, both comedies and dramas, are staged by professional theater groups in the major cities.

Dance

Filipinos love to dance and enjoy watching their country's professional dancers perform. They do everything from ballet to folk dances that often reflect Malay, Muslim, and Spanish influences. Most Filipinos learn to dance at home and rarely miss a chance to attend a village dance or a disco.

Beginning in the 1980s, ballroom dancing became a craze in the islands, taken up by Filipinos from all walks of life. They attend dances in hotel ballrooms, restaurants, schools and universities, and even in parks.

Many dance companies incorporated patriotic themes into their 1998 Centennial Celebration of Philippine Independence. For instance, Agnes Locsin created *La Revolución* for Ballet Philippines, the country's most renowned ballet company. The group performs both classical and modern ballet and integrates Western technique with Filipino movement, theme, and design.

The nation's most celebrated classical ballerina, Lisa Macuja, performs with Ballet Manila. Many other Filipino dancers have joined famous dance companies in other countries such as the Alvin Ailey American Dance Theater and the Atlanta Ballet in the United States and Ballet Ciudad de Barcelona in Spain.

The Philippines' most famous and decorated folk dance company is the Bayanihan Dance Company. It has been a source of national pride since its founding in the late 1950s, promoting the country's native traditions.

Folk Dance

In the *singkil* (above), an exciting Philippine folk dance of Muslim origin, a "princess" dances between moving bamboo poles held by boys or girls. Another bamboo folk dance, the *tinikling*, is inspired by the movements of a bird as it runs along the reeds.

A Cultural Mix   **105**

Many Filipinos enjoy playing musical instruments and singing. They learn both at home and at school and perform as amateurs at fiestas or in music contests on television. Professional singers and musicians perform folk, jazz, and rock and roll at clubs in the cities and towns. Filipino musicians are in demand all over the world, but many of the best prefer to remain in their own country. One of the nation's best-known folk singers is Freddie Aguilar.

Modern Philippine music is American or Latin American in sound and language. It often reflects romantic themes and subjects and has gained international recognition. Although Philippine radio is dominated by American popular music, stations are required to play Filipino songs every hour.

Classical music is performed in Manila mainly at the Cultural Center, the Metropolitan Theater, and the PCI Bank auditorium. Teenage Filipinos often win scholarships to study music abroad.

Ethnic music is often played at fiestas in villages and tribal communities. Instruments include Muslim gongs, the Apayao bamboo guitar, the local Jew's harp called the *kubing*, and the bamboo nose flute. The nose flute is played by blowing into the instrument through the nose instead of the mouth.

Pop singing stars are among the Filipinos' most admired role models, singing American pop tunes in Pilipino (or Tagalog) or in *Taglish*, a blend of Tagalog and English. Pop groups often use folk instruments along with modern electronic instruments.

One of the nation's leading popular entertainers is singer-actress Lea Salonga. She starred in the New York and London productions of the musical *Miss Saigon* in 1998 and 1999 after originating the role of Kim in the 1980s. She was also the singing voice of Jasmine in Walt Disney's *Aladdin* and the voice of Mulan in Disney's *The Legend of Mulan*, and she performed the song "A Whole New World" at the Sixty-Fifth Academy Awards in Hollywood. Bobby Enrique, known as "The Wildman," is considered the king of Filipino jazz.

Literature

Folk tales, myths, and legends dominated early Philippine literature, which was passed on to the young in the form of tales told by tribal leaders or village elders. The coming of Christianity to the islands was reflected in religious-based literature such as morality stories and tales of the lives of saints.

Before the nineteenth century, Filipinos were not allowed to learn to read or write. During the movement for independence from Spain, the greatest Philippine literary works were published. Most famous is the 1886 novel of poet-patriot Dr. José Rizal, *Noli Me Tangere* (*The Lost Eden*), which told of Spanish cruelty and Filipino hopes for freedom.

During the period of American colonization of the islands, Filipino writers began creating stories and books in English. Some wrote for art's sake, while others wrote to support nationalism and increase people's awareness of social problems.

Comic Books

Filipinos read Shakespeare and other classics, but many also enjoy reading comic books. Comic-book stands are popular in the cities, where Filipinos buy comic books to keep up with their favorite adventure, romance, or comedy serials.

Lou Diamond Phillips

American and Canadian movie fans know popular Philippine-born Lou Diamond Phillips from his many American films such as *La Bamba*, in which he played rock-and-roll legend Ritchie Valens, and the drama *Dark Wind*. He also made a big hit on Broadway playing the king in a 1996 revival of the stage musical *The King and I*. He was born in Olongapo, Zambales, to a Filipino mother and Irish father.

Movies

Philippine movie theaters primarily show American films dominated by sex and violence, but in recent years more Filipino-made movies that reflect serious local themes such as social conditions are being made and shown. Most American movies are shown and advertised in English.

Philippine-born Phoebe Cates is a popular movie actress in both American and Filipino films. Dina Bonnevie, one of the Philippines' most beautiful film actresses, has won many awards. Among the leading film directors are Lino Brocka and Briccio Santos, whose movies deal with social or political themes.

Sports

Basketball, jai alai, and cockfighting are the most popular sports in the Philippines. Basketball is a national passion, and Filipinos are considered to be among the best basketball players in the world. Basketball courts are found in every town plaza, usually beside the church and the town hall.

Opposite: **Basketball is the Philippines' national sport.**

From an early age, Filipinos play in or watch amateur basketball competitions, school championships, and professional and international contests. With a flair for theatrics, Filipino hoopsters frequently leap high and dazzle onlookers with speedy footwork and handwork.

Jai alai is a version of the Spanish sport of handball, played between pairs of players. A *cesta* (wicker basket) is tied to a server's right hand and he must hurl a hard rubber ball from it against a granite wall. An opponent must catch the ball in his cesta and hurl it back against the wall for the other player to catch and return. Points are scored when a player fails to return a service, either missing the ball or throwing it out of fair territory. The game is very fast, with hard rubber balls traveling at speeds of up to 150 miles (241 km) an hour.

Cockfighting is banned in many countries today, but it is very popular in the Philippines. Every town has a cockpit (*sabungan*), and excited crowds gather on Sundays and public holidays to watch and bet on

Basketball Highlights

The Philippines' national sports hero is Robert Jaworski, regarded as the greatest ever to play in the Philippine Basketball Association (PBA). For years he was the player-coach of Ginebra San Miguel, the country's most popular basketball team. At age 51, he played out his twenty-third season in the PBA in 1997, and he was elected to the Philippine Senate in 1998. The PBA Centennial Team won the twenty-first William Jones Cup international basketball tournament among Asian countries in September 1998.

Despite its cruelty, cock-fighting is a popular sport.

Filipino Stick Fighting

A sport little known by Westerners is Filipino *arnis de mano*, or stick fighting, which dates back to the conquering Spanish, who first banned it. The sport grew out of travelers who used machetes to defend themselves from robbers. Machetes are big, sharp knives used for cutting sugarcane and brush. The game is played with a 3-foot- (1-meter-) long hardwood stick *(tungkod)*. Opponents, well padded with headgear and chest protectors, are armed with two sticks and swing at each other until one player surrenders.

fights between two cocks. Not for the squeamish, cockfights involve a lot of pecking, clawing, and flying feathers until one cock subdues the other. Many cockfights are held during a single day's events, and thousands of pesos are won or lost.

Filipinos boast that they have more and higher-quality golf courses than any other country in Asia. Metro Manila is the golf capital of the nation with a dozen golf courses, while many of the islands have beautiful courses amid hills lush with coconut and pine trees. Several of the oldest golf courses were built by American soldiers stationed on the islands in the late 1800s and before World War II.

Camp John Hay Golf Course in Baguio

Life Stages

Several customs apply to important stages of life—birth, marriage, and death. After conception (called *naglilihi* in Pilipino), an expectant mother is *buntis* or *nagdadalang tao* (carrying a child). It is believed that a mother's craving for food influences the physical development of the fetus. The birth of a child is a joyful event not only for the family but for the entire community. Traditionally, many Filipinos celebrate the birth of a child in the family by planting a coconut tree.

Marriage among Filipinos is a sacrament and meant to last for life. Divorce is illegal in the Philippines. Most couples prefer a traditional church wedding. First, a custom called *pamanhikan* is observed in which the boy's parents call on the girl's parents and formally ask for the hand of the intended bride. As in America, the bride's family shoulders all wedding expenses. It is considered taboo for the bride or groom to leave the house the night before the wedding, and the bride should not try on her wedding dress until the morning of the wedding day.

Filipinos consider death the inevitable end of physical life on earth but also a prelude to a life beyond. A *lamayan,* or wake, is held for the deceased and food is served to those attending. The body is often buried the day after death, although this can vary. Mourners wear black clothing, and relatives of the deceased also wear a small black ribbon or pin. A nightly prayer, the *pasiyam,* or novena, is held for the departed for nine nights after the burial. After a year of mourning, the family offers a mass in the local church. Special visits are made to the grave on the deceased's birthday and also on All Saints' Day.

Horse racing also is popular, especially at San Lazaro in Metro Manila, with jockeys riding spunky Philippine ponies on oval tracks of sand. Some Filipinos play or enjoy watching polo at the Manila Polo Club.

Contrasting with the raucous arena of cockfighting and stick fighting, quiet chess halls are also popular. Filipinos, who play in their homes, clubs, and barbershops, and under mango trees in parks, are the most skilled chess players in Asia. The national chess hero, Eugene Torre, became Asia's first world-class grand master, winning over some of the world's chess superstars.

Filipinos practice martial arts such as karate, kung fu, and tae kwon do. The beautiful seas surrounding the islands make water sports such as swimming, diving, snorkeling, and fishing a pleasure. Mountain climbing and spelunking, or cave exploring, are also fun and exciting activities.

Daily Life in City and Country

These bicycle rickshaws
are used as a substitute for
school buses.

Daily life in the Philippines varies according to where people live. City life, village life, and mountain or coastal life can be very different. But close family ties are the common bonds among Filipinos no matter where they live. These bonds go far beyond parents and brothers and sisters to a broad extended family that includes local religious and civic leaders. Everyone cares about and looks after the well-being of everyone else.

Whether they live in the city or the country, if the family is Christian, everyone attends Sunday mass or a Protestant church service. Muslims gather each Friday, their main worship day of the week, to pray in the local mosque.

School Days

Filipino boys and girls must attend school until they have completed the sixth grade. They learn reading, writing, arithmetic, history, science, and other subjects just as children do in the United States and Canada. Classes are taught in both Pilipino and English. Education is free, and primary, or elementary, schools are found in cities, towns, and almost every village.

Opposite: **The *vinta* is a traditional symbol of the Philippines.**

Daily Life in City and Country **115**

Students attending a city school in Bohol

University of Santo Tomas students

Many Filipino boys and girls go to work after graduating from primary school. In the cities, they work for private companies, government agencies, or family businesses, such as small crafts factories, restaurants, or shops. If they live in a rural area, they may work on a family farm.

Filipino teenagers who do not go to work after the sixth grade can attend high school for the next four years. Most high schools are run by Catholic religious orders.

For those who can afford further education after high school, there are 63 universities and over 1,000 colleges in the Philippines. About 50 to 60 percent of Filipino teens go to college or university after completing the required secondary education. Filipinos are among the most highly educated people in the world.

The first university in the Philippines, the University of Santo Tomas, was founded in Manila by Roman Catholic missionaries in 1611. The University of the Philippines, the largest on the islands and supported by the government, was established in Manila in 1908 and moved to Quezon City in 1948.

Children's Games

Filipino boys and girls love basketball and kite flying. If an official basketball and hoop are not available, any size ball becomes a basketball, and a cardboard box or reed basket hung on a pole may serve as a hoop. Many children make their own slingshot, called a *tirador*, which is often their most prized possession. A stone shot from a slingshot can knock down ripe fruit from a tree, or a farm boy may use his slingshot to keep birds out of the fields.

While their parents watch cockfights, Filipino children stage spider fights and beetle jousts. A spider is caught, put on a stick, and pitted against another spider for a fight to the death. Small bets may be made on which spider wins.

Fat black rhinoceros beetles that fall off the trees are either kept as pets or used in a contest. First, one beetle is put on top of another. The top beetle tries to balance itself while the bottom beetle tries to run away. If the top beetle stays put, its owner wins. Beetles are also raced, but not for speed and distance. They start upside down, and the first beetle to turn itself right side up is the winner.

Filipino children also play games that have been traditional on the islands for years. In *luksong-tinik*, they jump over a playmate's outstretched hands or a stick. *Sungka* is a game of buried treasure in which shells or stones are put into holes and a playmate tries to find them. *Sipa* is a game in which players kick a palm or paper ball. Indoors, boys and girls play computer games, learn traditional crafts such as weaving or pottery making, and many learn martial arts such as karate or tae kwon do.

Jeepneys

After World War II, American GIs left thousands of jeeps behind when they returned home to the United States. Filipinos quickly claimed them, calling them *jeepneys*. They are painted bright colors and decorated to suit each owner, the gaudier the better. They have become the Philippines' taxis—the most common form of transportation on the islands. In Manila alone, more than 30,000 jeepneys crisscross the streets.

City Life

Young people in Manila, Cebu City, and other Philippine cities live much as their peers do in the West. They live in Western-style houses or apartments and enjoy all the benefits of modern city life. They have to contend with crowds, heavy traffic, noise, and pollution too.

Social life is more varied for city dwellers, since there are more places to enjoy music, go dancing, or attend sporting events than there are in the villages. Not every family has its own computer, but Filipino boys and girls are learning the new technology at school or in a community center.

Village Life

In rural farm communities, families live in small houses built on stilts to protect them from floods. Boys and girls work in the rice fields after school, riding the family water buffalo home at dusk.

After dinner, they join their *barkada* (playmates) and play basketball on the court beside the village church, or catch spi-

Ifugao boys riding scooters they made themselves

ders to use in spider fights. When their homework is done, they find someone with a computer or play Nintendo. Even people in remote parts of the islands have access to radios, television, and computers.

In the Tagalog families, children complete their basic education at sixteen. Their father then takes them to the village mayor, who is the local clan leader, to ask for help in finding a job.

Philippine Housing

Houses in cities are built of strong, durable materials such as brick or concrete blocks. They usually have two or three bedrooms and often have small fenced gardens. Larger houses and even some mansions are found in the suburbs. "Squatters"—unemployed people from rural areas who came to the cities looking for work—build homes for themselves out of scrap wood, sheet metal, and even cardboard.

In most rural areas, people who cannot afford to build houses of brick or concrete blocks do what their ancestors did. They build huts of bamboo and wood, raised above the ground on wooden pillars. The roofs are made of fronds of nipa trees, a type of palm. Nipa huts usually have one or two rooms reached by a ladder. Cooking is done outside, except in rainy weather.

Mountain and Coastal Life

Many members of the Filipino minority cultures live in the mountains, where each community may have its own language, clothes, lifestyle, and religious beliefs. Mountain children often help their parents by working on terraced mountainside rice fields.

Other ethnic minorities who live along the coasts, rivers, or shallow seas, such as the Bajau in the Sulu Archipelago, spend much of their lives on small boats fishing in the surrounding waters. Most coastal people, or lowlanders, are rural fishers or farmers, or live in cities and larger towns.

An Ifugao village in Banaue

The Banaue Rice Terraces

The Philippines have one famous landmark built by humans, the green-and-brown Banaue rice terraces. Located north of Mount Pulog in northwestern Luzon, the terraces have been called the "eighth wonder of the world." The terraces look like giant staircases 6,000 feet (1,829 m) up the mountainsides. Covering an area of 4,000 square miles (10,360 sq km), they were built more than 2,000 years ago by the Ifugao tribe. The descendants of that tribe still cultivate the rice terraces today.

Food

Filipinos, some say, eat not only to live, but to get in touch with their emotions. They seldom rush through a meal, because to them eating is a ritual that lets them touch base with family and friends. Food is served at most special occasions, from funerals to basketball games, and is always generously shared.

Rice is the Philippines' most important crop, and fish abound in the surrounding seas, so these foods are staples of the Filipino diet. At most meals, rice is served either boiled or fried with fish or meat. Rice cakes are a favorite dessert, and a Christmas favorite is *bibingka*—rice with coconut, egg, and milk baked in charcoal. Filipino food is a blend of Chinese, Malay, and Spanish cooking, but generally less spicy than cooking in other parts of Southeast Asia. Chinese food influences are a variety of noodles. From the Spanish came meat dishes with sauces such as *morcon* (beef with pork fat inside it); *pochero*

National Holidays

New Year's Day	January 1
Freedom Day, anniversary of the 1986 People's Revolution	February 25
Bataan Day	April 9
Labor Day	May 1
Independence Day, anniversary of 1898 declaration	June 12
Filipino-American Friendship Day	July 4
National Heroes' Day	August 27
Barangay Day	September 11
Bonifacio Day	November 30
Rizal Day	December 30

There are many American fast-food restaurants in the Philippines.

(beef, chicken, and pork pieces with cabbage and green beans); and *paella* (a rice-seafood-meat dish). America's culinary gift—hamburger—has become a staple of Filipino meals.

For city dwellers, where the pace of life is faster than in the villages or on the farms, fast-food eateries are everywhere. Besides native foods served by street vendors or at fast-food places, Filipinos enjoy pizzas, hamburgers, fried chicken, and hot dogs, most of them served at Pizza Hut, Wendy's, and McDonald's franchises in the cities.

Favorite fruits are banana, papaya, watermelon, jackfruit, mango, pineapple, guava, and native orange. These tropical fruits are eaten as both desserts and snacks. They are also used for medicinal and general health purposes. Papaya may be taken to cure constipation, and bananas provide good roughage.

Daily Life in City and Country **123**

Philippine Clothing

Filipino children and teenagers dress like children and teenagers in the United States and Canada—casually, and most often in blue jeans or cutoffs and T-shirts.

Philippine men also dress casually and seldom wear a suit and tie to the office. Instead, they wear long trousers and the *barong tagalog* (left). Known as the "Filipino shirt," it is a cool, semitransparent garment made from *pina* cloth, a fiber derived from the pineapple leaf and decorated with fine embroidery. Both the long-sleeved and short-sleeved versions are customarily worn over a T-shirt.

Fashions for Philippine women follow Western trends. On formal or festive occasions, however, women may wear the traditional *terno*, a dress with large, stiff, butterfly sleeves. Women in the cultural minorities often wear fancy hair combs carved from wood, horn, bamboo, and bone.

Drinks

A favorite Filipino beverage, a sweet coconut wine called *tuba*, dates from Magellan's arrival in the islands. Chief Lapu-Lapu served it to the Spaniards at a feast. It is alcoholic, which may be why Magellan and his men were defeated that day—they were tipsy on tuba.

In the northern provinces, sugarcane juice is fermented in huge jars that are then buried under the house to make a delicious wine called *basi*. Filipino beer, especially the San Miguel brand, is recognized as among the world's best. Soda and fruit juices are widely available, and coffee is more popular than tea.

Festivals

Every Filipino, no matter where he or she lives, enjoys a variety of cultural or religious festivals each year. In addition to Christmas and Easter, there are town or village fiestas honoring patron saints and other holidays that celebrate heroes or important events. They often involve parades with everyone dressed in colorful costumes, marching bands, decorated floats, dances, folk singing, and plays.

Filipinos dress in brightly colored costumes for the Sinulog Festival in Cebu.

Many young Filipinos and their families who live in the cities enjoy going to the provinces and villages during summer vacation, to see how others live in their diversified country. Rural families, on the other hand, enjoy visiting Manila and the other big cities. Families often escape the hot summer by going to the resorts in Baguio City, the summer capital of the Philippines, located on top of a mountain. The coastal regions are always popular vacation destinations for their beaches, water sports, and sailing and fishing.

Manila's best-known fiesta is the feast of the Black Nazarene. On January 9, thousands gather to carry a life-size statue of Christ made of blackwood through the Quiapo district.

Outside Manila, the most colorful fiesta is held on May 15 in Lucban, Quezon, celebrating the feast day of San Isidro de Labrador, the patron saint of farmers. Called *pahiyas*, the fiesta gives thanks for a good harvest. Towns on rivers or along the coast hold feast days with water parades.

At fiestas, special and very rich dishes are served to family and friends. The centerpiece of a festival meal is a roasted four-month-old pig called *lechon*, served with a thick liver sauce. Other favorites are *estofado*, pork simmered in burned sugar sauce thickened with nectar of ripe banana; *embotido*, meat roll stuffed with egg, olives, and relish mixed with ground meat and steamed; and *galantina*, shredded or diced chicken flavored with broth, milk, and spices.

A favorite fish dish served at fiestas is *lapu-lapu*, named after an early Filipino chief. It is a large fish steamed and garnished with mayonnaise, relish, peas, corn, parsley, and shredded carrots.

Opposite: **Preparing *lechon* for a Filipino feast**

Timeline

Philippine History

A tribe of Aytas (Negritos) comes to the **28,000** B.C.
Philippines from Southeast Asia.

Groups of Malays from Indonesia and **3000** B.C.
Malaysia settle along the coasts.

Philippine trade begins with China. A.D. **800**

The faith of Islam spreads to the Philippines. **1300s**

Ferdinand Magellan lands at Cebu and is **1521**
killed in battle by native warriors.
Miguel Lopez de Legazpi arrives in Cebu; he **1565**
becomes the first Spanish governor-general.
A Portuguese fleet arrives to challenge **1568**
Legazpi's rule.
Manila is established. **1571**

The Katipunan, a secret independence **1892**
group, is formed.
General Emilio Aguinaldo is elected **1897**
president of the revolutionary government.
Spanish-American War begins; Filipinos **1898**
declare national independence
from Spain; Treaty of Paris ends the war and
gives the Philippines to the United States.

World History

c. **2500** B.C. Egyptians build the Pyramids and
Sphinx in Giza.

563 B.C. Buddha is born in India.

A.D. **313** The Roman emperor Constantine
recognizes Christianity.
610 The prophet Muhammad begins preaching
a new religion called Islam.
1054 The Eastern (Orthodox) and Western
(Roman) Churches break apart.
1066 William the Conqueror defeats
the English in the Battle of Hastings.
1095 Pope Urban II proclaims the First Crusade.
1215 King John seals the Magna Carta.
1300s The Renaissance begins in Italy.
1347 The Black Death sweeps through Europe.
1453 Ottoman Turks capture Constantinople,
conquering the Byzantine Empire.
1492 Columbus arrives in North America.
1500s The Reformation leads to the birth
of Protestantism.

1776 The Declaration of Independence is signed.
1789 The French Revolution begins.
1865 The American Civil War ends.

Philippine History

Emilio Aguinaldo is elected first president of Philippine Republic; Filipino-American War begins. — 1899

Filipino-American War ends; United States controls the Philippines. — 1901

The Philippines gains commonwealth status. — 1935
The Japanese attack Pearl Harbor and Manila. — 1941

United States surrenders the Philippines to the Japanese. — 1942

U.S. general Douglas MacArthur returns to the Philippines. — 1944

Philippines gains its independence from the United States; Manuel Roxas becomes the first president of the republic. — 1946

U.S.–Philippines Mutual Defense Treaty is signed. — 1951

The Philippines becomes a charter member of SEATO (South East Asia Treaty Organization). — 1954

Ferdinand Marcos is elected president. — 1965

Parliamentary form of government is approved; Marcos declares martial law. — 1972

Martial law ends; Marcos is elected to a six-year term as president. — 1981

Marcos's opposition leader, Benigno Aquino Jr., is assassinated. — 1983

Widespread protests force Marcos to leave the country; Corazon Aquino becomes president. — 1986

Mount Pinatubo erupts, causing over 800 deaths and widespread destruction. — 1991

Fidel V. Ramos is elected president; treaty allowing the United States to occupy Clark Air Base and Subic Bay Naval Station expires; U.S. withdraws from both. — 1992

Government and Muslim groups sign an agreement to stop fighting and organize a self-rule region in the southern Philippines. — 1996

World History

1914 — World War I breaks out.
1917 — The Bolshevik Revolution brings Communism to Russia.
1929 — Worldwide economic depression begins.
1939 — World War II begins, following the German invasion of Poland.

1957 — The Vietnam War starts.

1989 — The Berlin Wall is torn down, as Communism crumbles in Eastern Europe.

1996 — Bill Clinton is reelected U.S. president.

Fast Facts

Official name: Republic of the Philippines

Capital: Manila

Official language: Pilipino; English is widely spoken.

A Filipina

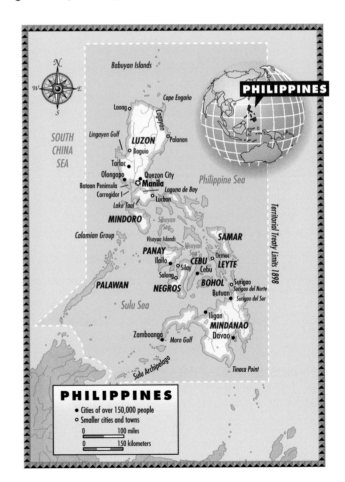

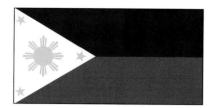

Flag of the Philippines

Official religion:	None; 92 percent Christian
National anthem:	"Filipinas," words by José Palma, music by Julian Felipe; Tagalog version adopted 1935
Founding dates:	1565–1898 as Spanish settlement; 1899 as Philippine Republic; 1901–1946 as U.S. possession; 1946 as independent Republic of the Philippines
Founder:	Emilio Aguinaldo, founder of Philippine independence in 1897
Government:	Constitutional democracy with two legislative houses
Chief of state:	President
Head of government:	President
Area:	7,107 islands; 115,839 square miles (300,000 sq km)
Nearest countries:	China, Taiwan, Vietnam, Borneo
Highest elevation:	Mount Apo, 9,692 feet (2,954 m)
Lowest elevation:	Sea level
Average temperatures:	82–92°F (28–33°C) in June 75–84°F (24–29°C) in December
Average annual rainfall:	35–216 inches (89–549 cm)
National population (1997 est.):	76 million
Population of largest cities:	Metro Manila: more than 12 million Cebu City: 3.1 million Quezon City: almost 2 million Davao: 1.3 million

Visayan Islands

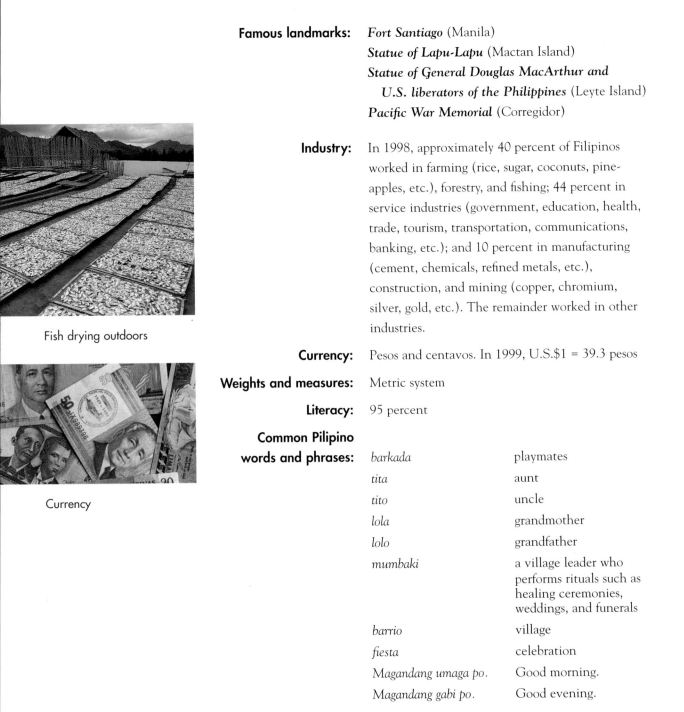

Fish drying outdoors

Currency

Famous landmarks:	*Fort Santiago* (Manila)
	Statue of Lapu-Lapu (Mactan Island)
	Statue of General Douglas MacArthur and U.S. liberators of the Philippines (Leyte Island)
	Pacific War Memorial (Corregidor)

Industry: In 1998, approximately 40 percent of Filipinos worked in farming (rice, sugar, coconuts, pineapples, etc.), forestry, and fishing; 44 percent in service industries (government, education, health, trade, tourism, transportation, communications, banking, etc.); and 10 percent in manufacturing (cement, chemicals, refined metals, etc.), construction, and mining (copper, chromium, silver, gold, etc.). The remainder worked in other industries.

Currency: Pesos and centavos. In 1999, U.S.$1 = 39.3 pesos

Weights and measures: Metric system

Literacy: 95 percent

Common Pilipino words and phrases:

barkada	playmates
tita	aunt
tito	uncle
lola	grandmother
lolo	grandfather
mumbaki	a village leader who performs rituals such as healing ceremonies, weddings, and funerals
barrio	village
fiesta	celebration
Magandang umaga po.	Good morning.
Magandang gabi po.	Good evening.

oo	yes
hindi/hindi po	no
Salamat po	Thank-you.
bahay	house
po or ho	sir *or* ma'am

President Aquino

Famous Filipinos:

Emilio Aguinaldo *Political and military leader*	(1869–1964)
Corazon Aquino *President 1986–1992*	(1933–)
Joseph Estrada *Current president*	(1937–)
Victor Gaston *Industry leader*	(? –1927)
Juan Luna *Painter*	(1857–1899)
Lisa Macuja *Ballerina*	(1964–)
Ferdinand Marcos *Dictator 1965–1986*	(1917–1989)
Galo Ocampo *Painter*	
José Palma *Poet*	
Lou Diamond Phillips *Actor*	(1962–)
Manuel Quezon *President 1935–1944*	(1878–1944)
Dr. José Rizal *Scientist, writer, political leader*	(1861–1896)
Manuel Roxas *President 1946–1948*	(1892–1948)

To Find Out More

Nonfiction

▶ Fernando, Gilda Cordero. *We Live in the Philippines.* New York: Bookwright, 1986.

▶ Gailey, Harry A. *The War in the Pacific: From Pearl Harbor to Tokyo Bay.* Novato, Calif.: Presidio Press, 1995.

▶ Hoyt, Edwin Palmer. *MacArthur's Navy: The Seventh Fleet and the Battle for the Philippines.* New York: Orion, 1989.

▶ Kinkade, Sheila. *Children of the Philippines.* Minneapolis: Carolrhoda, 1996.

▶ Lepthein, Emilie. *The Philippines.* Chicago: Children's Press, 1993.

▶ Nance, John. *Lobo of the Tasaday.* New York: Pantheon, 1982.

▶ Sullivan, Margaret. *The Philippines: Pacific Crossroads.* Parsippany, N.J.: Dillon Press, 1998.

▶ Tope, Lily Rose R. *The Philippines: Cultures of the World.* North Bellmore, N.Y.: Marshall Cavendish, 1991.

Biography

▶ Haskins, James. *Corazon Aquino: Leader of the Philippines.* Hillside, N.J.: Enslow, 1988.

▶ MacDonald, Fiona. *Magellan: A Voyage Around the World.* New York: Franklin Watts, 1998.

▶ Seagrave, Sterling. *The Marcos Dynasty.* New York: Harper and Row, 1988.

▶ Wakin, Eric. *Asian Independence Leaders.* New York: Facts on File, 1997.

Folktales

▶ Fernando, Gilda Cordero (editor). *The Culinary Culture of the Philippines.* Manila: Bancom Audiovision Corp., 1978.

▶ Hamilton-Paterson, James. *Ghosts of Manila.* New York: Farrar, Straus & Giroux, 1994.

▶ Robertson, Dorothy Lewis. *Fairy Tales from the Philippines.* New York: Dodd, Mead, 1971.

Websites

▶ **Philippines**
http://www.ldb.org/philippi.htm
Displays excellent links to Philippine websites on universities and research; media; social development; and culture, history, and travel.

▶ **Philippines.com**
http://www.philippines.com
Includes a great amount of information on the Philippines, such as news headlines and articles, a collection of links, a bulletin board to post notes, and real-time chat.

▶ **The Philippines—General Information**
http://www.dlsu.edu.ph/pinas/gen/
Provides past and present general information on the Philippines.

▶ **Philippines World Wide Web Links**
http://www.portalinc.com/~anton/toks.htm
Provides an extensive list of Philippine websites with information on government, travel, magazines, newspapers, sports, radio stations, and newsgroups.

Audio/Video

▶ *Asian Treasure Bag of Folk Tales.* Van Nuys, Calif.: Churchill Media, 1994. An enactment of Philippine and other Asian folk tales on video.

▶ *Collections of National Anthems, Vol. 1.* Hollywood, Calif.: Denon. A&M Records, 1990. The Philippine national anthem is included on this audio recording.

▶ *The Philippines: Pearl of the Pacific.* San Ramon, Calif.: International Video Network, 1996. A video visit to the Philippines.

Organizations and Embassies

▶ **Embassy of the Philippines**
1600 Massachusetts Avenue, NW
Washington, DC 20036
(202) 467-9300

▶ **Embassy of the Philippines**
130 Albert Street
Ottawa, Ontario KIP 5G4
Canada
(613) 233-1121

Index

Page numbers in *italics* indicate illustrations.

Meet the Author

I love writing for children even though I'm a bachelor and never had any bambinos of my own. I live in the Chicago suburb of Glenview with my dog Max, a mix of black Labrador retriever and German shepherd.

I began writing stories when I was about eight. I worked on my school newspapers in grammar school and high school in Chicago. While getting a degree in journalism at Michigan State University, I worked on the college paper. After graduation, I served for two years in the United States Army and was editor of the 3rd Armored Division's weekly newspaper, first in Kentucky and then in Germany. After the army, I worked as a newspaper reporter and editor, a magazine editor, and, for the past twenty-five years, as a freelance writer.

I enjoyed researching and writing this book on the Philippines not only because I learned more about the country's past and present, but because of the Filipinos I met. I did a lot of research at three local libraries in Evanston, Wilmette, and Glenview. I also got a lot of help from the Philippines Consulate in Chicago. The U.S. Department of State's Internet site provided me with latest census and other figures

and information from its Bureau of East Asian and Pacific Affairs. I met some very friendly and helpful Filipinos—some of them neighbors I talked to, and some I met on the Internet. On-line conversations with young Filipinos taught me more about their lives in the Philippines.

My published books for Children's Press include *Mikhail Gorbachev: A Leader for Soviet Change, Miracles of Genetics, The Video Revolution,* and *Lasers.* For Franklin Watts, I've written *The Black Plague* and *The Boston Tea Party.* Books I've written for other publishers include a recent biography of the actor Christopher Reeve, and I'm working on biographies of Princess Diana, James Dean, and Leonardo DiCaprio.

When I'm not at the library researching a new book, at my computer writing, or gardening, cooking, surfing the Net, or watching classic movies, I take Max for walks in the nearby woods or for a swim in Lake Michigan. Even though he's a senior citizen now, he's so happy when we're out together, he jumps for joy. Dogs and kids are the greatest!

Photo Credits

Photographs ©:

AP/Wide World Photos: 58 top (Joseph Capellan), 59 (Aaron Favila), 56, 64, 66 (Alberto Marquez), 18 top (Pat Roque), 46 bottom, 53 top, 55;
Archive Photos: 54 (Reuters/Erik De Castro), 58 bottom, 133 (Reuters/Enny Nuraheni);
Corbis-Bettmann: 48, 52, 53 bottom (UPI);
David R. Frazier: 100, 103;
North Wind Picture Archives: 42;
Panos Pictures: 77 (N. Durrell-McKenna), 94 (Marc McEvoy), 24 bottom (Marc Schlossman), 19, 23 (Chris Stowers);
Photo Researchers: 7 bottom, 38 (Gregory G. Dimijian, M.D.), 18 bottom (Bruce Gordon), 35 bottom (Tom McHugh/Chicago Zoological Park), 35 top, 36 (Tom McHugh);
Photo Resource Hawaii: cover, 6, 12, 26 bottom, 87 (John S. Callahan);

Photofest: 108 (Sam Emerson);
Robert Holmes Photography: 13, 24 top, 33 top, 45, 74, 83, 111, 132 top;
Stuart Dee Photography: 2, 7 top, 9, 11, 15, 22, 28, 31, 33 bottom, 51, 73, 80, 85, 88, 90, 91, 93, 95, 102, 105, 114, 116 top, 125, 127, 130, 131;
The Image Works: 69, 76 (Charles Steiner);
Tony Stone Images: 20 (John Callahan), 39 (Paul Chesley);
Victor Englebert: 8, 21, 26 top, 27, 30, 32, 40, 44, 46 top, 50, 60, 61, 62, 68, 70, 71, 72, 78, 79, 81, 84, 96, 101, 109, 110, 112, 115, 116 bottom, 117, 118, 119, 120, 121, 123, 124, 132 bottom;
Visuals Unlimited: 34 (Ken Lucas).

Maps by Joe LeMonnier.